Michael Gessner

SELECTED POEMS

FUTURECYCLE PRESS
www.futurecycle.org

Library of Congress Control Number: 2016942295

Published by FutureCycle Press
Lexington, Kentucky, USA

ISBN 978-1-938853-93-7

Contents

From
BEAST BOOK

From
ARTIFICIAL LIFE

From
SURFACES

From
EARTHLY BODIES

UNCOLLECTED POEMS

Acknowledgments

Foreword

Sometimes we see astonishingly clearly
The out-there-now we are already in

> —W.H. Auden, from "One Circumlocution"

The stones of kin and friend
Stretch off in a trembling sweat-like haze.

They may not after all be stepping stones
but you have followed them. Each strands you then

does not. Not yet. Not here.
Is it a crossing? Is there no way back?

> —James Merrill, from "Lorelei"

The Lorelei rock is the famous dark shale monolith on the bank of the Rhine River, notorious hazard to the shipping routes that use the river to ferry goods from the North Sea into the heart of Europe. Centuries of sailors have known these routes well, as did anyone associated with the rise of European industrialism. The lore of the Lorelei is the stuff of myth: many poems and songs note an eponymous woman who inhabits the rock; her song and hair distract the passing sailors, and you can imagine the result of distracted sailors and dangerous, protruding rocks in a river passage. It is an old story about desire and way-finding, and most of us will recognize its figurative shapes.

Merrill was a great poet of travel and myth. Of places over place. Seeing the world fresh, for Merrill, meant to move through it. Lush observations in his poems become a litany that seems impossible without the appeal of arriving and arrival's effect on the senses. It's difficult to think of Merrill ever assuming the stasis of one particular vantage; perspective in his poems and across them is part of the pleasure.

And so the first three couplets of "Lorelei" reads both as a sort of shorthand for a life's work and as *ars poetica*, replete with the terror and thrill of the unknown outcome. It would be a mistake to think that blur between writing and living unintentional; wayfinding is at the heart of both poem-making and the human enterprise. Our materials of course matter greatly, and ultimately dictate the ways that we eventually find. But we can recognize the premise of "Lorelei": the way is obscured, at best; at worst, unknown. We're following a path as well as we can, ultimately realizing we've extended past our comfort zone. In the poem, this literally leaves one midriver, wondering if the path one has struck is a crossing, and if not, if there's an out: "is there no way back?" If this were a blues song, we'd call this the moment we found ourselves at the crossroads. To paraphrase Auden: We may not know where we're going, but that not-knowing? We see that crystal clear.

To my ear, Michael Gessner's oeuvre chimes distinctly and gorgeously with Merrillesque tones, but piqued with Auden's love of the clear-eyed. This is a collection interested in way-finding across a life's work; it is Keatsian in its capabilities, both of the negative sort and not. The range in what follows is some of the pleasure and basis for my associative comparisons and echoes; consider the great Parisian sequences from *Transversales*; the animal that gets at the animus in us all in *Beast Book*; the inclusiveness of the poems in *Artificial Life*, domestic, spectral occasions for wonder and the pleasure of a poetic intellect in full form. *Surfaces* brings ekphrasis to bear, reminding ultimately that the way we see a piece of art and the attention we pay it is perhaps the same attention and earnestness we owe the everyday world, this everyday museum of our lived experiences. Finally, the poems in *Earthly Bodies* are also the early bodies in the oeuvre, and many signal as beacons the concerns that filter throughout Gessner's poetry: the domestic and the unfamiliar; the relationship between the banal and wonder; the shared public history of a place and the private moments that define our connections to spaces.

Robert Frost noted that a poem's shape begins in delight and ends in wisdom, a definition for poetry he clarified in his essay "The Figure a Poem Makes" by suggesting a poem as a "momentary stay against confusion." Gessner knows something deeply about this arc ("Is it a crossing? Is there no way back?"). Time and again, the poems work as stays against the relentlessness of the confusion of the world, a world with an eerie knack for racking up human-made catastrophes of increasing scale. This temporary art-made moment of wisdom is the narrative destination of even the most lyric of poems, and it is a destination to which Gessner frequently brings us, poem by poem, across the collection. Consider this final section of his poem "The Masters," a poem that observes group of schoolchildren visiting the Fitzwilliam Museum in Cambridge:

> The teacher went on to explain
> how artists live in a different world
> when they work, a sacred place
> and how the lives of the children too
> could be the same, whatever their direction,
> whatever they made, how the things
> that surrounded them that day
> were forms of affection, and the masters
> themselves, objects of imagination.

The "stay against" here is both literal and figurative; it is a form of affection, and an object of the imagination. Time after time Gessner's poems in this collection beckon us to lean in, listen close, requiring attention. Frequently in their closures they cinematically zoom in or pan out, focusing us on details of either minutia or scale; the universe in the quarter note; the personal revelation out of the vastness of the cityscape.

Just as frequently the invitation to attention is offered in the music of the language. Consider the intoxicating concluding sentence across the final three stanzas of the marvelous "Fireflies at Harsen's Island":

It would never happen again, not like this,
& it did not happen, so they settled in
for their stay—the immediate signal:
the popular ode turning on itself
like a leaf, a dove's wing, the wind dipping
into the waters of old ports & clouds
like the colonnades of Smyrna shifting
to accommodate them, for those few

who alerted others, altering them,
blips like the shouts of city boys
at summer camp into the dark meadows,
the bending neon silos, the ballrooms
with balconies of bright ideas,
dithyramb of lantern-glow, cold sulphur
spirals of nymphs performing in the shapes
of their shapes, heads filled with divine objects,

one moved forward into the immense dark
as Zelus was led past the port & the last
sphere of influence, forsaking all others
on the journey of no return, the bold
voice exchanged for a dawn of ghosts,
they returned to Bar Harbor, Twin Rivers,
the one fawn-eyed farm boy with the fruit jar
lantern & seniors in their gilded buses.

How can you resist the consonant tug of wind and wings and water, of clouds and colonnades and what accommodates them? Sulphur spirals performing in the shapes of their shapes? Ballrooms with balconies of bright ideas? Of influence forsaking? All of it welcomes you, reader, in the romp of the poem's occasion. Gessner's deep sense of language and music sets off how the boys of the poem assemble just as the chance occurrence of the lit flies themselves, a happenstance occasion of magic, connecting us to a history laced with Zelus and Smyrna and all the ports of our lives we fly past. And then the moment, like the occasion of the poem, is gone: we're back to our mundane dailiness, our Bar Harbors and Twin Rivers, perhaps changed, the thrill of the fruit jar lantern full of fireflies lasting only as long as they do. Magic is wild, difficult to predict or keep; Gessner's deft touch proffers the same for music—it is wild, difficult to contain in the mason jar of the poem's shape, and yet there it is, a sweet dithyramb lantern that lights a way.

I'd be remiss if I did not note Gessner's deep sense of compassion everywhere apparent in these poems. If way-finding is the heart of these *Selected Poems,* with music and attention as the most prominent modes, compassion is one pole around which the poems constellate and map. Consider these heartrending lines from "For the Innocents at Sandy Hook" that somehow help manage our public and private grief at the incoherence of that violence:

> Classrooms emptied of children's things,
> paper and paste, and love's imaginings,
>
> bundles of peace, Christmas-blessed
> with the unborn and the dead at rest,
>
> nothing can reach you now, not lead or steel
> or what life itself eventually reveals.

Rage is simple, and therefore often not interesting in poems; grief is deep and deeply human, and attaches us, Gessner seems to suggest, to both our past and our future. It is Auden's sense of the clear-eyed bearing on that which is so difficult and heartbreaking to see clearly. This, too, the poem reminds us, is a part of the world in which we live.

Or these lines, from the astonishing poem "Anorexic Student," where the limit of compassion is made in clear in the limits of language—both what we have the power to say, and what we can't; where we have the power of agency balanced against those things that are beyond our control:

> I cannot speak for you.
> You will remain your wish,
> Something left unsaid,
> Obsessive image, in five years
> At the outside by physician's count
> Those studio teeth will calcify
> Hard as stone—the heart gone—
> And I will insist I have some voice
> In the matter, asking
> For what you would only scorn,
> Some small honor grieving still.

What is remarkable in both "For the Innocents at Sandy Hook" and "Anorexic Student" is the manner in which Gessner chooses compassion in the face of knowing the ultimate pointlessness of that choice; still it is preferable, still compassion matters above ignorance, even though we know fiercely what we are powerless to change. What ultimately matters, the poems suggest, is that we choose to recognize suffering. And through these poems, it is hard not to recognize that Gessner has made a type of grace, something durable and as complex as the violent and complicated and periodically incomprehensible world in which we find ourselves.

And yet: sometimes we see astonishingly clearly. This is a remarkable body of work, work that delves deeply into the ways in which we become ourselves. Each poem is a record of a life's work in poetry and reveals some-thing of the human enterprise. They are the ways, ultimately, that Gessner has found. So, back to Merrill: Is it a crossing? Is there no way back? The Rhine is a big river, but I would sail it with Gessner any day.

—Tyler Meier, Executive Director, University of Arizona Poetry Center;
former Managing Editor, *Kenyon Review*

We dance the beach,
our soles tingle, clouds roll
over & over, darkening
the sand, we pass flash-mashers,
beat-up bodies, gagging spectacles,
spiny blowfish washed up with other debris,
bent nails, rotten wood, algae-sick-of-sea,

& dance on, you with your green eyes
& wild hair, you with your many selves,
rounded sea glass, double rainbows,
a central self we share in coyote
& cactus, & others, unnameable,
you introduce me to everyone new,
& what will become of me is you.

From
TRANSVERSALES

(BlazeVOX Books, 2013)

Paper Moon

Art gives form to the invisible. —André Malraux

It has been my wish—rather it has been desire's wish—which I have
called mine without understanding it, tho' it is desire nonetheless,
as if I am desire speaking, & desire has led me to the desk of the
concierge, Rudi, at Hôtel Saint Dominique to ask how to access
the roof to get a better view of this section of *7ème*. No, the elevator
goes only to the fourth floor, & access to the roof is by stair & for
the maintenance staff only, so you can't go there. Didn't I see
workmen only this morning, taking up materials? They are building
something on the roof, yes? Hmmm. This is not generally known.
We do not want to disturb our visitors. Maybe it is an addition for
storage, maybe it is scaffolding for repair, or maybe it is a work of art,
a diversion for the guests. Here Rudi gives his perfunctory smile & returns
to the paperwork on his desk.

Across the street in O'Brien's Irish Pub, I imagine the form of the new
work—a diorama—*bricolage*—interior oscillating walls—& with
a surface like the surface of the paintings I had seen recently in art
museums, the minute, geometrically symmetrical crackling of say,
Tiepolo, a parchment, like the back of my hands, (only a recent
development), the texture of the materials through which we inhabit
this world & which assume us into the world of cooperative conditions
which is taking place now, as it has always. Even if we only imagine
its knowing, as we are known by it, source & field of dissolving renewal,
always attracting us somewhere.

Sometime during the next Guinness Stout, which, if taken after fasting
for several hours, has a smoky finish on the palate with a curiously
suggestive edge of chocolate-charcoal, & some chatter with the bar host,
there is my Corona, a Cubana Romeo y Julieta from the *tabac* shop
which the woman retrieves from a glass case, & since I've become
a regular customer, she pinches the foot to know if it is dry or spongy,
smiles over her shoulder, & continues down the row to find one sufficiently
resilient, which I now smoke half in & half out of the open shutters—
I may sit on a chair positioned between O'Brien's floor & the sidewalk—
still looking up with an occasional caress at the back of my head, a palm
of air—as if I could see something on the roof, & seeing only the workmen
enter & leave the building with more materials—& since it is early
evening & I have been up very early thinking about the scaffolding,

making some notes for another project—all the projects are poems as it
turns out, or some connections among them as if they are reaching out
to embrace each other—the word 'project' is used only for my dear friends
who do not care to understand poems & would make an issue of my interest
in them, an entertainment among themselves—& smoke the Corona down
to its bitter leaves, which puts me in mind of the leaves of Daphne, when
pursued by Apollo, transfigured into a laurel tree, *Laurus nobilis,*
of all things, & thus those leaves in Picasso's "La Femme au Feuillage,"
& the history of memory in my hand, then return to the hotel room to lie
on the bed where I am swept up in sleep still imagining what art is taking
place on the roof, imagining ascending stairs.

Woman with Leaves

—La Femme au Feuillage, *Picasso, plaster, 1934. Private collection.*

Objet de rebut. Let not even fools fool themselves,
the pregnant tension underlying the page; the pages
that flit about the mind, thin leaves on display
like thin skin that breaks with age & blood cracks
& Amazons flow. These things slide along the page,
& open paper-thin wings, bat & butterfly, thin fingers
of the hand, caressing carp, the fish's fins, (the woman's
shoulder on the dark steps of the Metro in Seine-Saint-Denis
flipping mutant flesh-leaves for coins), the outstretched fist,
the sign of protection & threat the runaway has assumed
in her leaves, invitation to the House of Image, the Biological
Theatre, leafy Eros, a welcoming that cannot be entirely
withdrawn, & thus the display of violence is saddened
& weakened, & the girl-tree imagines she has become
part of the canopy, the boxy head, a camera recording
everything, the mouth a cave, the tongue a bell, the heart
that beats out words for the heart's tongue to tell, the mouth
full as if volume itself, the vowels alone, swollen leaves,
were mouth's meaning, & other leaves, those on the branch
over the breast shiver on apart, alone.

Place des Vosges

for *Michel Moisan*

In the oldest square in Paris, in the Marais, a monument
is being built, a monument to all the monuments,
greater than any, a monument to the culture of invention,
invention transformed, a monument grander than the Panthéon,
that final cradle built by the masons of the Creuse.

It is a perpetual spiral turning ever upwards, revolving with murals
commemorating those who made Paris, the Paris of the senses, who
maintain it and keep it alive, without which there could not be
another Paris, there could not be the musée imaginaire, and here
in this square there is a spiral of revolving images and colors unseen,
for those who put ideas into the geometries of materials, the creators
of Lescot, Lemercier, Haussmann.

Without the labor of the unknown there would be no grand palais—
no grand e'toile—no grand boulevard—no grand bibliothèque—
no grand basilique—no grand école—no grand arc—no grand jardin—
no grand menagerie—no grand institut—no grand académie—no grand
cimetière—no grand tour (with its 72 gold names)—no grand musée—
no grand cité de lumière—

No, no Louvre, no Orangerie, no Orsay, no Musée des Beaux-Arts
no Sacré-Cœur, no plaque with gold lettering for Apollinaire above
the brasserie, no stone for Éluard, no name on Hugo's door, or the door
of Gautier, no Bateau-Lavoir, no 27 rue de Fleurus, no Sorbonne,
no Odéon, no home for Dior, Guerlain, Vuitton, no Sainte-Chapelle.
And they, the builders, too poor to live where they build, build always
for others, homes for others, memorials for others, statues for others.
They build and repair and serve and then return by night to districts
outside the Paris they built and where they cannot live.

Ceinture Rouge, noose of Paris.

To them, in this oldest square in Place des Vosges, their monument
will exceed all others and will overshadow the statue of Louis XIII,
and will draw its energies from the vigor of the builders and from
the spirit of communes and from the descendants of the Communards,
defenders of Paris, and this turning narrative of murals in colors
yet unknown will be seen only by the pure, the poor, the laborers,
and will outlast the Panthéon and the venerable entombed
therein.

Rain

It's been raining all day, raining in suburbs & in city parks
& continues in sheets across avenues, stalling traffic,
bouncing in waves off glacial curbs, & will, in turns,
reduce itself to a patter, then to finger-taps—tap—tap—
tap—drops down gutters & down spouts, only to gather
strength for the next downpour or the next—raiment after raiment—
breaking levees, flooding villages, sweeping them out to sea,
it is raining somewhere always, even now the rains rain on tin sheds
& tile roofs, it rains in the barrio & in the banlieue, & in the financial
district, rains rain on the roof of le Moulin de la Vierge & the lovers
who wait inside, & it rains on the steps of Montmartre, & on the
abandoned convent in Seine-Saint-Denis, over the chartreuse lichen
& the ochre lichen on stone walls, but here this morning it is raining
over my house, a monologue of rain, & therefore it is raining too
where you are, & the rains are not the tears of infant angels
for our world's sake, they are not the rains of Zeus, or another god
inseminating the fields of Mother Earth, or clouds of science, they are
the patterings of an unknown companion, lost & distant, now returned
to wrap this house in sheets of itself.

The Markets of Seine-Saint-Denis

The Metro shoots out of Paris—an eel through
a winding cave—gaining speed, the urgency to get
to where it must go. In the crowded car we grip
the balance pole. There is a gang of boys
who stare at us as if we were invaders, ghosts
of one tyranny or another, come back to haunt
(*honte*) with another plan for oppression.

    November 23-27, 1870

> *For two days Paris has been living on salt meat.*
> *A rat costs 8 sous.... Pâtés of rat are being made.*

    December 1, 1870

> [a friend] *came to see me today. We ate bear meat.*
> *—stag, and bear, and antelope—presents from*
> *the Jardin des Plantes.* [La Ménagerie]

                      —V. Hugo

We hurtle on toward the end of the line and deboard
at Seine-Saint-Denis. The boys are the first off, and wait
on the platform for the new arrivals. One will shout to a
woman stepping into the subway—she has lost something,
and must attend to it—while she turns, and the doors are
closing, another boy grabs her purse as the doors shut
and the train pulls away. They run up the stairwell laughing.
We pass a mutant mother on the stairs under a light like an egg
in a wire cage, dull in the damp passageway. She sits hunched
by the wall. There is a rusted can for coins by her feet,
and a baby cradled in her lap. She stares into the eyes
of the subway voyeurs, exposing her right shoulder;
crossing her breast with her left hand, she flips
her fingers at the three fleshy fins from some aberration,
thalidomide, or a remnant of the aquatic life.

    December 24, 1870

> *It is freezing. Ice floes are floating down the Seine.*

December 31, 1870

> *Yesterday I ate rat. We no longer have horse to eat.... I am*
> *beginning to suffer pains in the stomach. We are eating the*
> *unknown.*

January 3, 1871

> *Moon. Intense cold. The Prussians bombarded*
> *St. Denis all night.*

Here we've come to the home of the homeless, Séquano-
Dionysiens, the grounds of the kings and queens exhumed
by revolutionaries, come to the labyrinth of tented markets
that sell living creatures for consumption, what creeps or runs
or crawls; crickets, monkeys, turtles, horse organs, pig intestines,
insects—siege food—meats of unidentifiable origins, carp
and eel and octopus among jars of chamomile flowers,
vanilla beans, hibiscus leaves for bissap tea; absinthe
leaves for licorice tea. This is the motif.

January 12, 1871

> *We had elephant steak for luncheon today.*

We cannot stay long, never after dark, the guide shows us
the Basilica of St. Denis and hurries us along to the markets.
They are festivals of brightly colored tents with every exotic thing
the heart desires. We must hold our belongings tightly to our
chests, leave no thing loose or it will be ripped away, never
look eye-to-eye for you may become prey, put your cameras away,
hide the slings, hold your handbag to your body. Do not reveal
your hands or let them hang by your sides.

We walk about the edge of the rings within rings of booths
packed together, we could go deeper but it was not advised.

It was not advised by the concierge at our hotel in Paris,
not advised to come here in the first place, and we went anyway,
and we did not know why. During our walk from the Basilica
to the market places, there was an interview. What did the
foreigners make of this region of the Red Belt, how startling
and varied, how multicultural, how novel. It was as if we

did not know poverty; that we were charmed by cheap rugs and scarves, underwear, motor oil and mouse traps. This was televised on France 24; later, a German affiliate ran the interview with background footage of the fires set during the last riot, as if poverty is uncommon, when it is everywhere.

Some streets are named after Communards, and others who served the Paris Commune; Jean Baptiste Clément, Gustave Courbet, Louise Michel, Jules Vallès.

Le Select

Almost every afternoon from spring to fall she may be
seen at the same table ordering the expresso first, then
a Malbec, or two if it is a good day, or if it is a bit
brisk, or if it is drizzling over the canopy, otherwise it's
the whites, especially during the summer months.
The order is followed by a silver cigarette & she allows
the smoke to drift upward casually from open lips,
otherwise she appears distant & indifferent. In this way,
sipping from cup & glass, two hours pass. Her gloves
are black gauze & she is here owing to a moderate
inheritance; for many years the absentee proprietor
of L'École de Charme for privileged girls of subdued
energies, now mothers with summer homes on the coast.
Just down the street at another café is a man her age.
He wears a white jacket. They share the same condominium
building & do not know this since the building is imposing
& they are in different wings. Although here they share
the terrace of pavement. He is a retired officer of foreign
affairs. They will never meet; they would only see emptiness
in each other, when they would rather see the sleek, the curious,
the slight splendors, emaciated models, petty scams, & other
nuances of the street.

Communards

In the spring of 1871, and for about two months following the Franco-Prussian War, the National French Guard made possible the establishment of "The Paris Commune." When their countrymen came to collect cannons and machine guns, the Guard barricaded the city. During "Bloody Week" it is estimated that 20,000 to 50,000 of the French Guard were executed; others were later imprisoned or deported to forced labor colonies. The Commune became a rallying cry for the working class.

Here they are again, the faithful dead.
They could be anyone, Spartans or Serbs,
Fenians, Nigerians, the "Freedom Fighters"
of every land, but these are different.
They have been uploaded for the world to see,
torn chests, disfigured faces, black and white
daguerreotypes, nude bodies on display,
electronic images in digital perpetuity.

They have been disgraced forever this way,
all bearded and boxed, subjects of one last
macabre prank or hoax before the grave.
They lay uncircumcised in their cheap board
caskets in rows set at an angle for the camera's
best exposure, some with black wreaths
pressed into dead fingers, held over hips,
placed around genitals as if in mockery.

Most are young as war dead are, and once bold,
without compromise, and their loves were set
aside, having taken up a cause that was
unattainable and basic as bread, slain by countrymen
as much as irony, and in these photographs
remain an epitaph to the strange prospects
of victory, more obscene than any corpse could be,
ideals torn easily as a body,
a body torn easily as a spring plant.

Le Moulin de la Vierge

In the mill of the virgin, the local patisserie,
lovers wait in line with their loves,
they wait for *mille-fueille,* the buttery brittle
thousand sheets with layers of light cream whipped
silly with the scent of raspberry,
for pastry cones and pastry shells,
of spun fluff in glass cases so they cannot float
away, & chiffon slippers lined with lemon froth,
bowls of macaroon puffs airy as cupid's cheeks,
& when the lovers are in love they are in love
with Paris, Paris glazed, Paris powdered,
Paris of flaky cream horns,
Paris of vertiginous confection,
Paris Paris pastry crust.

Theatre

Tonight it is theatre & it is theatre only. It is the culture of spectacle.
It is what is on the marquee. It is the theatre of bell ringers, of grand
boulevards, the chairs of brasseries turned toward the street, toward
the promenades of pedestrians, the flowing scarves, the diatribe,
the sweat of speakers on the concrete stage of persuasion. It is the night
of the illusionist, the one black leaf stuck to the pavement with rain.

The mural of history is theatre, the gold statues in city squares are
theatre; the churches, theatre, the military in their engagements & in
their parades, the dramas that take us in, surround us, & promise
liberation, & so it is always, theatre marvelous, theatre compelling,
theatre corrupt, the monk in his cell in love with pity & martyrdom
is the theatre of the one soul, tremulous leaf, the floating self, artist
& diplomat, the industrialist & the national community, all theatre,
but for the act of labor alone without consequence, for the anonymous,
not as lawyers live in the theatre of fabricated character & political
trial, eruptions of mountains, as if in rivalry with panoplies of cosmic
displays, cataclysms, flamboyant effusions & death star collisions,
& tonight, here now, always, there is the theatre of the poet & the poem.

The Keys of Paris

The lovers write their names on locks
then fasten them to the black chain-link fence
on both sides of the *Pont des Arts,*
that wooden footbridge over the Seine.

There are rows & rows of lovers' locks,
the chromium latches glint in the sun,
& the lovers, in a grand gesture of fidelity,
toss their keys into the river, & depart.

The keys lay on the bottom, sometimes turning
in wreaths of current, or they may remain
still for years, or they may roll,
crossing over one another.

The Abandoned Convent at Seine-Saint-Denis

Doors.

The guide must pound and pound on them until the edge
of his palm is flushed with pounding and the guard leaves
his station to unlock the wooden doors, centuries old, tall
and gothic and black and set in fluted channels in an arch
far above us. The doors, reluctant, creak, and the guard
seeing his counterpart, the guide, motions us in. The doors
are closed and will remain closed until we have seen the nun.

Courtyard, the lichens.

Lichens, the lichens, chartreuse lichens and yellow lichens.
Rings circling over rings. Deckles of rust lichen and rose lichen
on the courtyard walls, deep golden lichen in miniature sunbursts,
walls crusted with splotches of lichen, *croute de pierre.* They are
everywhere; over the fieldstone courtyard, about the metal spouts
up which cats shimmy to stalk the window sills for the sparrow too
sick to fly. The window has a blue frame; there the keeper tells us,
the old woman looked out every day at the workers who passed her
way, who occupied the apartments once inhabited by the sisters of St.
Botanica. The lichens create their own designs, seek their own
symbiotica, joining filaments, extending themselves into shared identities
by texture, the unknown chemical callings of algae, even the purple plaque,
isolated on the dry stone fountain. When the workers returned, the last
nun would still be staring from her window, staring at the courtyard, the
opposite walls, the lichens, staring at space itself. One morning they
filed by and she was no longer there. The keeper maintains the empty
apartment now, cleaning the glass daily.

When it becomes dark the lichens sink into the darkness. The few
black pocks, the teals, dark to darker blue-green, the grays, are
the first to go, the rest surrender, glyphs in ink into nightfall, nightfall
and the moon, and as the moon moves its light ricochets in
phosphorescent tracers, glimpses of silver bloom on walls,
the courtyard, the metal spouts, the locked doors.

Père Lachaise

Leaves clatter down cobblestone streets like tin cups,
& empty souls move about the Sunday children
who laugh & chase each other down the streets
chattering after themselves, they give half-life
to this city of images, human & divine,
where no one lives & no one dies,
where families collect their young
at the end of their visit, & leave this place
to the leaves that swirl in wheels...

When Mars, the Gorgons, Lamia,
& the warheads are sleeping,
& I am vacant, no longer thinking,
when all things are absent,
you arrive, a ghost anthology written in the dark,
of other lives, lovers, & lovers' art.

Wilde's Tomb

But these, thy lovers, are not dead....They will rise up and hear your voice...
and run to kiss your mouth. —The Sphinx

In the garden of Père Lachaise,
city of the dead, we passed angels
covering their faces in shame,
& nineteenth-century trees, with tops bowed
as if their only purpose was to grieve,
& crossed the Transversales to Wilde's grave.

When lovers leave, they leave their kisses
glistening on the gray slab,
on impressions of lips themselves,
a tissue of strangers' cells
the conservators cannot leave alone,
& scrub the graffiti, as the plaque decrees
by law, no one can deface this tomb,
& still the images of lips remain,
dark gray stains of animal fat
imprisoned in limestone.

Lips are pressed as high as lovers
climb, against the Sphinx's ridiculous
headdress, on the carved trumpet
of fame, & on the cheeks of its voracious face
of mindless passion flying with eyes pinched tight,
that some farsighted lover tried to open
with lines from a red pen, like a blepharoplasty,
while others kissed its sybaritic mouth
to make a poem a prophecy.

So here is love alive
surviving the wreckage it survives,
a lipstick envelope of hearts on their flight
to some other place, less aware,
more receiving, a final Champ de Grâce.

The Return

With a tour group closing in, we left Wilde's sphinx
where sentiment always is, & followed the Avenue Circulaire
to the wall of the Communards, then to a bench across from a cenotaph,
broke a baguette, & stared as mourners stare.

Behind the bench, a grassy hill, & behind it, a boulevard
we could not see, but from above, over the tiers of trees,
a French girls' choir gave its rehearsal from some high-rise;
angled notes folding & unfolding purely on decisions of air,

& went on like this for an hour or more, the repertoire
complete, the girls with ribbons in their hair, as if performing for
Experience for its own sake, bounced down stairs
to waiting cars, cafés & girly affairs.

Evening came. What was left but the long walk back,
a decanter of wine, house red, in one of those cafés on Rue Cler.

Petits Cailloux

The planter above Stein's headstone holds small stones.
We looked about until we found two smooth agates on the
ground, one black, the other amber, and set them in place
with our left hand like ancient Jews, to mark the place,
to say someone came here and someone thought of those below,
for Gertrude at her best, for Alice tucked in back without a view
like misplaced punctuation, and we prayed our prayers for what
lives souls take, for bad winters, dusty apartments, war, shabby dress.

Staircase at Sceaux

—Mon projet aujourd'hui est d'être absorbé.

In the window of a shop in the *Passage des Panoramas*
(next year it could be Prague, Budapest, or Riga), the onlooker
with the cape over his arm, exposing a lining —it has been soiled
—stares at Kertész's photo of a staircase in Parc des Sceaux,
all but a ruin now, what memory left in exchange for silk ball
gowns, early evenings & gelatin-silver passages, & the partygoers,
each with a long-stemmed flower with glass petals, float about
the scene in black & white, mouths open in phatic chat, the moment
eternal in the open mouth, glass heart of history, they glide on invisible
rails up & down the steps meant to take strollers from lower
to higher ground & back again (in this park designed by André Le Nôtre,
Atget, a compulsive photographer who wished to gather every image of Paris,
also took photos of steps like these, but not from this angle of abandonment,
with such an abundance of curled leaves, & never as haunting). For now,
there are the faces of passersby on the surfaces of bubbles passing
over shop windows, rhizome of reflections in the eyes of the onlooker,
which are eyes of mirror, faces floating over walls of polished granite,
across the glass roof of the arcade itself, the revolving images of strangers
where he has found a home among the homeless, having become them,
the city, the freedom of interchangeability, lost identity, album
of the arcade, a renewed body, Dreamer of days.

Glossolalia

In the columbarium of dead tongues,
each in a glass box with a bronze plate
stamped with the indecipherable
name of its owner, I can only imagine
how they howled over the ruins of past ages,
with the certain knowledge
their words would be kept
in the ancient libraries of Sumer or Ugarit,
in languages now lost or forgotten.

Even tonight, somewhere there is
a gospel tent, or a caravan stopped
for a meteor shower, to form a circle
on a mountain slope babbling
scrambled syllables, as if the dead
languages had returned, eloped
& married in multiples,
polygamous echoes on a journey
trying to make themselves known.

Voltaire's Cap

A student with time to kill
between classes, I dallied underground
in the Detroit Institute of History
where I found Voltaire's cap
in a glass case in a corner
with other embroidered objects
of the period. It was white cotton lace,
like a skull cap. It would fit a baby's head.

I, too, have hats, a rack of them,
straw for summer walking, the black band
stained with streaks of salt, a worn Panama
of my father's, some tennis caps,
& a dark blue felt for winter wear.

We could walk the museum in our hats,
walk the long halls, discussing perfection
over & over, then take the escalator of hats
to the garden floor café known for its pastry
& discuss the rich imaginary girls that show up

between classes, & your cap, the size of my fist,
empty of longing, & how the history of all things
is a collection made of such things.

Film

The thin, multi-chromatic skin of bubbles is film's cast, the oil
slick on the water's surface from the power boat ride you took
one evening with a friend I can't remember, on webs that span
docks & doors, the sheen on costumes of improvisation, abandoned
corpses, on tree & trunk, flossy reflections from moods of weather
& light, the film that joins film when surfaces caress or collide,
the film we see, the one of ourselves, slick celluloid, the iridescence
of the oily film on our skin, how it beckons & floats with untraceable
turnings, coppery nuances in the gold haze about the summer stream
at evening, the film of memory memory makes, glossy photographs
in plastic albums, the gleam of new book jackets, shiny pages of birds
& beaches, the surfaces of objects, seashells, a ring, shimmer of lip
gloss, the silk shirt I wore last night, luster over morning moss,
the surface of the moon.

Poem

One thing alone does not exist—oblivion. —Borges

The poet in a lawn chair by the side of the sea
had been reading another poet, perhaps Neruda,
and since it was summer and languid, and he had been
reading a long time, he fell to sleep.

When he woke, he called out to his wife to tell her
his dream, and when she did not answer, and no
one was about, and the house was empty and there was
only the sea, he took his pen and wrote:

The poem is always its own. It is true and it cannot die.
At our own death, from the chest, the treasury
of the poem, a baby dove, invisible,
flies out to find its flock in eternity.

Letter to a Poet

Permit this brief intrusion
into a life of uncommon callings,
simply to say what I read this morning
shimmers like the gold foil musings
in the compositions of the Masters
of Sunlight, its memory reflects
in my palm, flake of tremulous gold.

Moonstruck

At 2 a.m., Irish paces the hall.
I hear her collar tags when she shakes
and she shakes every few minutes
due to the fullness of the moon
my wife claims, and there is no place
where the dog is at rest,
not in her bed at the foot of our bed,
not on the couch downstairs
or in my son's abandoned room.

Maybe it is the moon pulling us
away from ourselves, an agitation
of the central nervous system. We, too,
are awake tonight and though we do not
pace the hall, we are restless
like the dog who cannot sleep,
and imagine a state of consolation,
a return to dreams: the silhouette
of Irish against a gray dawn dancing relevé.

The Poem of Death

This is the poem of death.
There is only one
and no other.

Every one is an occasion,
one way or another,
and the last poem is this poem of death.

It is an occasion like no other.
I will no longer lope after elegance,
beauty's body, or love's wonder.

I will be sorry for everything
I was, and for everything I was not.
I speak to you as if you were my brother.

I will forgive everyone.
Death will make this possible.
There will be no other.

Death was in the mind
before thought or love,
in ourselves, and in our lovers.

The poem of death is speechless.
A companion will appear again
like another self, like your brother.

Enough now, enough has been said.
The spinning leaf will spin
like no other.

I Had Your Book

I had your book in my hands.
It told me everything about you,
the thin pages of the heart, the harried life,
and why you left yourself
for the time it took to create another.

Your book and I are the same,
like the peach blossom god
who wants to be created over and over,
who is silent and cannot say enough.

Just as memory surrounds devastation
making a loveliness of disaster
that floats over time like blossoms
over homes hurricanes collapsed,
or kaleidoscope dew over headstones.

When print vanishes, the stitching separates,
when the title fades and is no longer readable,
the knowledge of your book is in my hand,
the impression of the spine in the palm remains.

Boy in a Boat

The boy in the boat did not care
if he said the right word, or if a word
was said, if he moved, or if he did not,

reclining on the bow, indifferent,
as if enigma never seized him,
his eyes still covered with morning glaze,

adrift in the Pacific inlet, on still water
into the evening, & every evening
was the same.

He wore my father's oversized shirt,
& like my son, we sometimes shared
that long & distant look of distraction.

There was this & something more,
I would always envy,
love, & never understand,

in the boat he did not care
if he worshipped me
or some other minor god of the air.

Six Spanish Girls on the Streets of Cambridge

Here for their summer programs,
to speak household French, or English,
they come arm in arm
chatting down King's Parade,
in the evening, after dinner,
& laugh together over the bridge of Cam,
then turn down a narrow street,

& I follow, leaving my own turning
far behind, in the plume of exuberance,
as if I were absorbed in their company,
before they break up, enter Clare College,
& go to their rooms,
leaving the street & all that's in it
resounding with girlishness.

French Tile

The tenants next door are re-flooring their apartment
with porcelain. It is midnight-blue with sprays of silver
dust scattered here & there, as if looking down
on constellations.

In the evening when the tenants, a childless couple,
hold hands, objects among objects, they must imagine
themselves floating among endless stars.

The Masters

Fitzwilliam Museum, Cambridge

After rows of cuneiforms pressed
in salmon-colored clay, after exhibits
of gold-foiled glass on glass shelves,
aisles of marble heads, abducted thinkers,
and foreign patriots, cases
of painted fans and samplers
ancient girls made, after the displays of swords
and hammered armor pilfered from lands
philologists could not name,
we saw a group of children pass
under the Caryatids, then gather
in Gallery Three. All in red vests
and white collars, some stood, attentively,
others sat cross-legged on the carpet
faded with floral designs, a few on settees,
listening to their teacher explain how
the creators had affection for their art,
otherwise how could their art be?

The sunlight through the clerestory above,
suffused the plaster frieze, a cast
of the Elgin Marbles, and onto scrolled frames,
poppy head finials, and entered
the pores of statuary, the faces
of ancients, the flying creatures
of myth they made, and the red-vested
children, respectful, clean, as if the sun
was slowly purifying everything.

The teacher went on to explain
how artists live in a different world
when they work, a sacred place,
and how the lives of the children too
could be the same, whatever their direction,
whatever they made, how the things
that surrounded them that day
were forms of affection, and the masters
themselves, objects of imagination.

Circulation

I am certain of nothing but the holiness
of the Heart's affections... —Keats

The rounded heart's rhythm keeps momentum
with the cosmos; they are the same.

The wounded heart does not understand
circularity. It does not know sameness

even though they are one. It does not understand
the affection of death.

Washed Out

My father stands in boxers,
back to the sea. He holds
my hand. I am five. We are a pair
on this Florida beach. We've remained
for years this way in black and white.

At forty-seven he looks "washed out,"
a phrase I learned from him,
used by a generation without pigment
spray, or tanning booths, to explain
the pallor of the face in age,
its waxiness from lack of circulation,
its corollaries in cotton fabrics hung
too long in the sun,
or what hurricanes do to ports,
and the conch on the beach
bleached of color.

He was no longer "in the pink,"
as his childhood chums would say
of each other when flushed
with health and expectation,
but not washed up, either,
not like the bloated things
that bellied-up and were pushed
away by tides, the undesirable
forms on the sand we stepped around.

Still we are here,
squinting against the sun,
still casting shadows.
In a few years I learned another phrase:
"Life is cheap," he'd say,
odd for one who held it so near.

Ferns: A Study

From his pose in the garden
just as his voice became
my own Froebel stepped into the evening

of my dream for his uncommon love
of the young and with his notes
at the close of another century
collected from an elemental source
of children, my children of the forest
and the perpetual lily pond mad for the end,
playing and sometimes translucent
against the sun endowed with beauty
which has become commonplace
and for beauty's tension they never cease
from the pursuit of themselves
as though they inhabit this place
only to breed themselves to death by error.

As forests were once ferns
and ferns infant in the dumb morning
existing of notions
which were also geometries
copious among us

as they were always among us
even in the dreams of twelfth-century girls
dreaming at the edge of the forest
in anticipation of the unimagined season,

the caress and the still life
of ferns
on seacoasts and on the white porches
of summer homes
or hung from the platforms of wooden depots,
how they bowed along the boulevards
welcoming victors to the city,
and atop cool Corinthian planters

in the lobbies of grand hotels
there were ferns

in the background of photographs,
pharmacies, and funeral parlors,
and in the corridors of museums
positioned carefully below milky skylights
that are sealed and permit no entry,

but most in a memory of children
there were ferns
copious, still and sometimes swaying
in the settings of their stories,
in the stories of their sleep.

Toth

In the ancient Egyptian pantheon, the cult of Thoth,
the god of scribes, writing, & other dominions, was not
extensive. Seshat was his female counterpart.

After all these years you would think
that you would have written to me,
to send some assurance that after
an honorable life,

I will not have to pay the ferryman
more than once, that I will be
judged worthy of some small grace,
a favorable review
where it counts, a reader or two
once I have passed, diviner of magic
& time, the moon, most underrated
of gods, I relate to you,
figure on my desk all gold & black
with head of the sacred ibis
(your bill competes with your stylus),
be there at the weighing of my heart,
let it be no heavier than the feather
on the opposite scale
so that it won't be cast away
nor saved for some future life
such as I have known,
rather allow this soul
to live in fantasy, a dreaming
head in a dreaming dormitory
of wonder & felicity only
like some protozoan mindless of itself
among kindly forms all color & warmth,
say, eternal, glowing voyagers
complete with present sense,

without conscience or the grief
of this earth, let me be
without the need for words or pen,
or reluctance, or bread & bone,
or this world, or friend.

Seshat

I have seen you bathing
in the river under the moon,
Mistress of the Long House of Books.
Has your companion told you
about me?

      Has he?
How I passed the test.
How my heart weighed well.
For this, surely, you, the loveliest
of your kind, could place a volume
of mine in a secure archive to be present at the unveiling
of the next universe,
or the next, complete, divine.

Winter Reading

The historic church packed, the poet,
famous, congenial, mythic, & singular—
the atmosphere warmed by adulation
& after the last applause
faded into the dome of the nave,
& the spectacle
& spectators disappeared,
out on the cold pavement
in the parking lot
a crippled girl
who had put on lipstick
& rouge for the occasion,
in a wheelchair
surrounded by other students,
the teacher who brought her,
before she was lifted
into the van,
said, "Yes, I can do that.
now I know what I want
to be," holding her manuscript
up to the moon.

Walt Whitman's Novel

It is a Vivaldian summer passing
in verdant flashes, chlorophyll cells trembling
from rapid growth, then a child
comes to the door, she will uproot
weeds for a fee. At fourteen flat-chested
& podgy, her parents, working people,
promised her a horse on her twelfth birthday,
a companion. They have yet to make good,
& so she tells me of her newfound calling,
she will draw the heads of horses,
travel from stable to stable,
she will do this for a fee.

How do we ever find our way? Must we each
have a labyrinth? An impossible design in green?
Walt's first book was a moral illustration
on intemperance & by the author's account
written in three days inspired by gin.
He did this for a fee.
From my window I see the child
who wants to travel town to town
in the garden pulling weeds.
I tell her she can stop,
pay her off, enough for a box of charcoals,
some paper, acid-free, well-made.

Looking for Picasso on eBay

My wife loves art. It is her birthday.
Because of this, I am looking for Picasso
on eBay. Among the thousands
of lithographs signed & numbered
in pencil, I find "Paloma sur fond rouge,"
& bid the balance of my bank account.

Now I am in electronic Picassoland,
among the mixed media, how prolific
he was, & varied, & how unlike
the literary artists, bound to one voice,
denied their periods during a life,
confined so often to a single genre.

But this does not matter to my wife.
She will frame this tortured thing
I have ordered, praising Picasso,
his artistic gluttony, his infant self,
how he left his true believers, the women,
a man after his own heart.

La Belle Époque

After a fine arts degree from a college
with a name like a flower, my sister
worked for an art dealer until he went
out of business, and is now employed
by a local delicatessen owned by the same
person who owns the meatpacking plant
where her son works, finishing a GED.

All the art in the world cannot feed a table,
she says, you are with the voice of your age,
or you can talk to yourself in a corner. Take it,
or leave it. This is no Belle Époque. It is political,
which means the beast is in costume. Read Vico.
But cultural values are recursive, aren't they?
I ask while she works on her son's hair,
shaping it into midnight-blue metallic spikes.

Sex Education

Like I tell my students, sex
invigorates. It is what we are
supposed to do with our lives,
but with caution. Use caution
like the colleague across the hall
who teaches punctuation, wondering
if a comma splice is more dangerous
than a colon. Then let go. And just
don't go out on the make, looking
for someone to bugger for buggering's
sake, make it mean something. Not like
that fuck of a swimming coach—who
should have been arrested years ago—
jumping into every pool, as if through
decades of countless affairs,
nameless faces that come & go,
you could keep yourself decent, complete,
not a mockery to self & soul.

Gold Stars

My niece won a certificate for gymnastics.
She is ten. Now she wants to be world class,
like the girls on television. I was the same way,
until my knee blew out, then I discovered
piercings, & now my goal is to have a studded face.
I get a discount because I work at an ink shop
& there's lots of trade going on. I could be
lizard lady. Who knows? Besides, even if you win
a gold medal in an event, unless you have
the personality to go with it, & become a broad-
caster or something, people forget. Like it goes down
a black hole. Don't tell this to the up-and-coming.
Most of the would-be's can't win for losing. Maybe
this isn't true for artists like my boss, but in sports,
it's different. Who's going to be vaulting when
they're fifty? Find something you can keep going with.
Besides, getting trashed isn't so bad. I tell my niece
I could get my boss to do her first tat for free.
Even stars trash themselves.

Cigar Rings

Even now they are evidence of paradise,
paper bands kept in a favorite drawer,
fathers once gave their children to be worn
as rings, a convenient source of early
mythology, the Dutch Masters in their best
black puritan hats gathered around
a table discussing art, no doubt,
the Da Vinci brand for creative men,
Pleiades, with a smoke destined
for the stars, & the royal bands
of American Indians holding clumps
of tawny leaf on either side
of an earthly globe over which Indian
Tabac ruled, & other myths too, Excalibur,
Romeo y Julieta, Montecristo, White Owl,
& promising a smoke affectionate
& amusing, Sancho Panza Extra Fuerte.

These exist in a pure state,
free of toxins, cancer, grief,
calmed, hand-rolled, leaf by leaf,
chaste as the flower-women framed
in circles of gold foil, Flor de This
& Flor de That, Flor de Fantasie,
Flor de Forever, Athena of the Cameroon
wrapper & spicy ligero filler,
a smoke for the wise, & on the walls
of cigar bars, floating with his silken harem,
the sultan of smoke moves in clouds
from the best puros, judiciously holds
his Cubano Pilato, & the whole ensemble,
vessel & feathered fans, everything
carries the odor of rich exotic flowers,
& the women, Flor de Murias, dark
beauty with ringlets staring at her one
flower, pining for her lover,

the big-breasted Belinda
of the full-bodied double corona,
& her opposite, the pasty ingénue
who would date anyone, up for sale
on every Gloria Cubana, they could be
married for an hour or two, rescued
from a cellophaned life
by sliding money over a glass
countertop, beauties existing in wreaths
of smoke, sandalwood, burnt cherry,
notes of butternut & leather, on back
porches, & on summer evenings,
in the rings fathers blew for their children.

Passion Bracelet

A friend of mine was accused of infidelity
by his wife. He claimed it was her fault
for suggesting the passion bracelet in the first place,
the one that would re-energize their relationship.
After all, it was a balmy day and they were strolling
hand in hand through the mall when they found
the stand and inside the glass case was the bracelet
that would change their lives. It was incised
with symbols from Atlantis, made of zinc, copper,
and tiny magnets to transform those ozone ions.
It was all too much, he explained, too much to control.
Passion does not know direction and that is why it is blind.
He asked for understanding, sympathy, time,
and while his wife was considering late that night,
the passion bracelet glowed when he went outside.

Geographics

On a switchback in the Catalinas we stopped
to catch our breath, leaned against our walking poles,
& to our right, upslope, a triangle of grasses
& shrubs with a dark streak from the melting snow,
of two months ago, a *mons veneris*
that arcs & swells in spring, & this suggested
other formations: burial mounds that take the body
in whole, phallus of saguaro cactus,
clitoral pedernals, crooked thumb mountain,
the finger lakes, tulip head beach, crested butte,
crevasse & hoodoo, fertile crescents, colonic caves.
It is not always sex, but sex is what we see,
deltas where waters meet,
Psyche's shared symmetries.

Magnificat

The greatest statement ever made,
the *magnum opus* of all things,
is the manifest of desire.

Desire the perpetual, desire
the profound, the everywhere,
texts whistling
in the trees of Ceylon,
blowing up gulf coasts,

desire in the heart that ceases,
still as red coral, made so by it,
and in the heart that remains,
and in the dissolving pool
after the rain and in the rain.

It is the dumb giant gone
to the children's tea party,
the return of the lava avalanche
and the rarest mountain flowers,
the tsunami that washes out
generations, whole islands.

It is the earthly organism
cooperating with systems
here and beyond the moon,

while we stand, desire itself,
forever awash in bright danger.

The Innocents at Sandy Hook

Nothing can reach you now, not lead or steel,
or what life itself eventually reveals.

No more studies of kindness or courtesy,
not grace or charity, all is needless now.

All is needless now, sky, world, family
grieving for their bundles of purity,

now beyond disgrace, failure, winter streets,
of whatever attacks, and then retreats.

Classrooms emptied of children's things,
paper and paste, and love's imaginings,

bundles of peace, Christmas-blessed
with the unborn and the dead at rest,

nothing can reach you now, not lead or steel
or what life itself eventually reveals.

Somewhere, Days

Somewhere, the days
are white gloves
floating in silence,
waiting to be occupied.

From

BEAST BOOK

(BlazeVOX Books, 2010)

A Suite for the Four Primary Animals of Passion

Greed:

> Gold heart. In the condominium of luxury,
> among overstuffed pillows
> there is the heart of pity & fear,
> the black heart from which all of us
> suffer. Emptiness. Something was taken
> from us & cannot be recovered.
> It is the source of all aggression.

Lust:

> Red heart. When dancing with another
> I dance also with myself & what is now
> mandatory, passes, only to return
> again; the compelling *entrée* that takes
> us up those weary steps
> to the event which notes its passing
> even as it is passing.

Beauty:

> Blue heart. The sum of the pageant
> & the parade is always the same & there
> is no place to turn once ruin is understood;
> that it is wished for by others,
> the admirers, & that it will arrive no matter
> what, & just as blessings rise in favor,
> suffering grows too & follows behind, disguised.

Permanence:

> Invisible heart. The condition is irreducible.
> I am with you always & was never
> a thing outside itself, zoo or carousel,
> but for you, & all the others, after you
> had gone, & all that was before
> anything arrived, before movement
> was noticed, or heart's beating.

Heart-Eater

The tip of the Forest Elephant's tail,
(adult swampgorth, or flying chimera),
is spade-shaped; red heart/black heart.
It is the heart of the Lamia,
that Queen of Shark hearts,

tail-tip, or cartilage-shape of the stingray's
hood, the water's pterodactyl,
who feeds on adolescent love,
eating the exposed heart

& transforming it to its root,
the killing shaft, the serrated pike
that shoots through the diver's skin.

It is excess,
a dose greater than needed or good;
heart eating heart.

The Thousand Consolations:
Notes on a New Year

It is the time of year when temple bells are rung.
They are heavy & black with pollution,
with dragons and lotus intertwined.

There is a gong for garrulity,
one for sarcasm, another for pride.
There is a gong for greed.
For vanity there is a gong.
Deceit & fraudulence, there are gongs for these.
There is another for sinister calculation, & one for regret.
There is a gong for every sorrow of the human heart.
Gong over gong, they echo over each other, a doubling,
as the old fades into the new
until the Buddha bells recant
all 108 defilements.

Then silence.
It is the New Year.
Now is the Future of Things.

In the Future of Things
I will not want.
There will be no Valley of Death.
Those whom I love will not suffer.
I will never be alone.

Obstruction, a Monody

This is not a moral tale.

The house on the hill
must be transparent
or it cannot be a house.

Perspective is obstruction.
It looms like the Colossus of Rhodes,
blocking new light,
or those cosmic giants, black holes,
feared devourers of Arion
containing unseen sylphides
of antimatter —the man-eating tree
of Madagascar—to swallow
unknown galaxies whole—

Without perspective art cannot be technique.

While monsters wrestle,

the house on the hill
must be transparent
if it is to be a house.

Mythos

Spring, & hummingbirds
whiz by the mollusk head,
creature of myself,
echo & air,
clumsy-hooved psyche,
heart of Wexford green,
by the rising of the moon,
outfitted for convenience,
in an appearance
that prances & cowers,
prates about the menagerie
with the accomplices of a plot,
a chain of deliquescent selves,
just as the hummingbirds arrive,
in circles broken by abrupt
distractions, when every observer retreats.

Accomplices

They seem compatible,
companions even, honor
& revenge, for instance,
camouflaged in the park,
& the triplets; vulgarity, spectacle,
& self-promotion, with a singular
bright face, another example
of the existence of the polycephalic
found in most species; deception & love,
(all forms), purity with its double,
loathing, or deformity & justice,
or those bearing the soft down
of agreement & conciliation, the politicos,
& the most genuine, the contemptuous,
bearing quills, (porcupine, hedgehog,
Echidna, spiny rat), or those stingers
on the webbed feet of the platypus,
or those in the zoo
of lofty principle, & their offspring,
ridicule & remorse, & when all
is shaken & then abandoned,
when torment has ceased
for some other thing,
there is disengagement
from all discord, a settlement,
the vacant stare,
& there are always
the special ones, selections made
in the dead of night by criteria
unknown to the public, the cohorts
we find so often in manufacturing,
tourism, commerce, fair trade,
a political model, like oil, squirting
out of the machine, arrogance & cynicism
attending a luncheon with platitudes,
& across the expanses of the great
deserts, there are caravans

of the commonplace, with creed
& cause & flag,
throngs of newborns
in a mall nursery
as if they were their own
family crying in unison,
& our belongings
given to coteries; water circles
invading others & thus, never
entirely ourselves, unless left
to the undistinguished presence
of that form which never had identity
but which we know is ours & ours
alone, belonging like another body
equal & invisible with our own.

Matching

The current of air
that sweeps cold across
my deck one morning is this.
Or, say, a world
brighter than my own
floats to mind,

& I have stepped outside
the self & into another
zone occupied
with foreign sensations only,
like the mourning dove about the house
flown inside.

Evening of a Satyr

It is the classical hour on cable,
the girl in the off-white, tattered dress
coiled on center stage in blue darkness
has become herself faun & afternoon.
Bluer shadows move over drapes & floor,
like the flute's wood-notes through which she weaves,

a reaction to displace the evening
meeting, hers was the form she had assumed
for nothing more than this, uncoiling
herself upward in a spiral, fingering space
for some transparent film, in pursuit
of essence; how we judge the body's worth.

Canticle, Poet-Anima

It was a strange awakening
that moved from place to place
staring at itself
like the first thought of the body.

The birds stood on the roof,
waited in the rain
& belonged to no house.
There was cold music

in the spinal column
from the city & from the plain,
shuddering at dawn & at sunset,
prosperous as one thought

                    I was Paris

                         & I was the Serengeti

White Doors

Always there was the dumb look of animals,
the black and stationary eyes
of the field mouse, rabbit, or sleek ferret
fixed on nothing, or on destruction.

Still they were vulnerable
as in their movements, clumsy,
or swift with elegance & desire,

imagined spirits who could not speak,
quiet as innocence walking alone
or the sea turning inside

the sea around the summer pavilion
at the end of the pier where the water
tugs at the pilings to dispose
vagrant, vendor, or financier.

The sea, clumsy in its pulling
as a dumb lover trying
to own & be owned
by the creature of desire.

Tesla's Pigeon

In the Hagia Sophia
I saw Tesla's white pigeon
circling upward
in the Great Dome
where everything is said
to hover,
where recollections dim,
& joined her in her radiance
like Zeus, whispering over & over
that I was him, Nikola, her lover.

Conscience

(Satyr to Nymph)

Conscience sleeps with one eye open,
a notorious omnivore
consuming everything in its path,
good intentions, trust, the ultimate
relationship. A gaping orifice,
it will eat it all, & praise itself
with sickness.

Today it feeds on grief & pride,
& tomorrow, denies itself
to create regret & longing
for its inwardness. Like BASILISK
it can kill with a glance.
When it has achieved its highest point,
it collapses, & waits for itself,
a victim with one eye open.

Sylphs

In essence, the SYLPH is a wisp
of air, deliquescent, sometimes
colored by reflections of sun
glinting off particles of ozone
& oxide in the troposphere
which is their habitat, & may seem
as slips of pale pink, or pale gold,
or opalescent,
or never appear to appear at all.

They are simple presences only.
When not resting in thermal hammocks,
or attracted to the pleasance
that emanates from musings,
they are taken up by GUSTS
& blown about, or they may drift
in the trailings of clouds,
or descend; breath of bee
& butterfly, turn white
& float as caddisflies do, or dally
in the vibrations made
from hummingbirds' wings.
They are a confusion
to HYDRA & MANTICORE.

INNOCENCE has named them;
Chance & Gesture. Frailty.
Glimpse & Vision. Purity.
Paradise.

In dissolution, wind & water
conspire to replenish another,
unknown to the thing itself,

& thus the SYLPH is parthenogenic
& this accounts for the continuation
of their simple presence,
these wisps of air, with or without
color, or direction.

Manticore Speaks

HYDRA, you overrate me
& I am nothing like you imagine.
I cannot use my teeth as arrows,
or change into other creatures,
nor do I have your impossible head
for things.

It is not true; I do not consume
carousels of sylphs
like white flies about some food source.
The villagers gave me extra powers
from frenzy & fear. I offer the certainty
of horror, night-stories around fire pits,
& caprice. You are no match
for me, tho' I stay away from water,
the vipers, magic trees,
& live for what men see in me,
what they most admire in themselves,
vigor, gallantry.

Parthenogenesis

from Hydra

CLONING is not new
& has been observed repeatedly
in the formicine ant, the scorpion,
Hammerhead shark; in Flora,
the Komodo dragon, who gave
a virgin birth to eight on Christmas,
& in the human species;
in Agnes of God, St. Clare
of the Flowering Rock, & Mother Mary,
all reproduced without earthly mates,
although pregnancy is a hardship without an accomplice

& occurs in other conditions as well,
in suspicion, or fear, these are communicable
& repeat themselves in others,
& once they assume shape, continue.
In this way are they given life,
go on the prowl, like MANTICORE.
When they recur, come home, so to speak,
they may take up with others,
a synthesis, & it is how we account
for our changelings, our other selves
like the voice we cannot quite recognize
but must search out, join, to become
what they are.

The Blue-Eared Homunculus of Expectation

cannot be tamed.
It is wild always,
bound to Exhaustion,
each a keeper & slave to the other.

They cannot see
the benefits of sitting alone
in a vineyard, or being with Landscape
until they are breathing it
& so they dance with confusion,
hold hands with the clatter
that excess brings
& invade every absence.

Excitement alone is purpose.
Infants are taught this condition
from the beginning by well-meaning adults
who wish to entertain themselves
& believe they are communicating joy.

Some conditions cannot be cured.

This Was an Evening

from Spectre, a Sylph

This was an evening that will remain
in the mind of memory
itself, will stay like a ghost image
through rain. It was determined to be
so from the beginning.

The shelves of clouds with gilt ledges,
the volumes of gray in shifting dimensions,
appear only to reappear changed.

And the people, the people were inside,
gone to their rooms. The streets
& the air were gray & gritty
& I imagined myself drifting
over the bodies of those I've loved
or those I imagined I loved drifting
over their faces & hands until dawn came again
& the night was only a missing thing.

Ineffable Conversations

All right Leonardo
so the hairs of the ox are alive
& the scrolls of animal skins
somehow sense the words written on them.

Do the morning leaves
above the buried dead
hold an unaccountable breath?
Is the current moment round?

Is this what you mean?

Enough for Einstein's universe
to reside on a curved plane,
what ancients knew in the figure eight
on its side, seductive as an expanding
polyverse of sense, an evening out on the town,
Odalisque reclining on her lounge.

Robins' eggs in the pockets of boys,
broken wheels & grain silos in fields,
spires that vainly exclaim their point,
cathedral vaults, the human forehead, planets,
& Leonardo, even the shape of your eyes,

this geometry does not surprise,
or for this, we search for a symmetry
not our own, another longing to be told.

Ars Memoria

Slender summer classic
what would you make of me?
Or what would you have me make of myself?

Something cold, I suppose, in stone
memorized until there was only the dark
face of an ancient moon.

Confession to a Girl

I want to become your life
because your future is all that is left.
It is what I was.
You are the subject of myself,
thus you represent everything.

If I am grief, I am my own memorial
& see you by a wall of ivy talking
to a friend, or reading in a café,
or staring out at the rain listening
to music, the music of the world.

To you forever of the nineteenth year
I am jealous of your life just as I am
jealous of the lives of the dead.
I am the vampire of time,
voracious, I consume culture.
This is my Valentine & my sin.

The Girl's Reply

I have always found your admiration
attractive, but I think you act in haste.
You haven't considered everything.

There have been others, short-term affairs,
maybe you have suspected this.
Still, you remember me, after all—
& don't think I haven't noticed
how much you sound like me, as if I could love
you back to life again and again.

I've seen you watching me from a distance
like a timid voyeur dreaming
of what it would be like to take my heart.
Your intent is clear as day.

As for your age, it doesn't matter,
you are an exception—like me,
gods and days have their personalities
and I have mine—imagine me
going on like this, but I've been waiting
to go somewhere exotic,

maybe a little extravagant. I am fluent
in French, but as I've said, I've been waiting
for you to say these things.
I want to hear them again.

Stranded Cat

The cat in Lucien Clergue's *Eros and Thanatos*
lying on the beach at Saintes Maries-de-la-Mer
is only a half-decomposed corpse filled with sand.

The body resembles a piece of macabre iconography,
a stone *transi* with some fur still left along the spine,
down the striped tail curled like a long finger
as though to summon another image, here, it is
the photographer, Lucien, to make posthumous
meaning, a look, a life story—

She must have wandered out during low tide
pawing for shellfish on the sand bar and there
dallied too long, or in the lulling monotony
of the salty air, napped, and dreamt of crustacean
fantasies prancing past in improbable shapes
and floral colors. Her jaw, open and fixed

suggests she woke too late and cried to breathe
a final request, ignored, the oral cavity
holds the amber froth like a cup of champagne,
an offering for the anger of the sea, the sudden
tide, a coastal storm, an outburst, and the body
molded into the sand as though to deny

destruction, the rigid image of the thing,
a white eye, a necklace of foam, another
form that requires dissolution and absence,
the water becomes gentle as the hands of Antigone
in this moral dream of nature—itself dreaming
the personification of the scene by the shore—

so far as wind and water and sand agree
to focus in the production of being's text,
the burden of animation and the void
for an onlooker to accept these views, anger
alone, or benevolence to cancel the original image,
then all complaints are unjust and retracted—

The cat in Lucien Clergue's *Eros and Thanatos*
lying on the beach at Saintes Maries-de-la-Mer
is only a half-decomposed corpse filled with sand.

Commemoration of a Tongue

Facile switch, first fragment of happy thought
wedged in the slick saline of brimming ardor,
in meringue then, in shellfish bisque, Chablis,
or in any other, numbed between
with sorbet clemencies,
consumer of the living you earn
is pure sensation, wrapped around the premium
Honduran with Sumatra leaf, richest member
of the club, you have suffered a case of disaffection,

guest speaker for the moon,
and the high court justices,
reduced now to salt or spice, heat or cold,
dull, overworked, insensate,
like a verb of a forgotten language
left drying on a desert rock—
target of the heart, as for memories,
tongue, you should survive all others,
left alone, composed, entire, the only one.

Necessity

from Impulse, a Nymph

Necessity cannot live alone
& is created by other conditions

that are themselves created
by a central organizing authority,
an obligation seen in daily needs,
food & water, shelter & sex,
& if exceeded, are poisonous,
& if neglected, the same.

Even a mother of invention
must have parents;
compulsion & delirium,
the pistons of celestial physics
& therein an epistemology
which is, above all, the lyric
& this is the new morality.

The lyric rests in locations,
& only appears during necessity's
lapse from its own tensions
as in meadows smeared
with yellow flowers,
or landscapes of Indian summers,
the balmy air where we counted
our youth & where there was no
other thing but the golden lens
& the ghost moon.

Rites of Spring

Leave it for Poliziano to praise
    These figures from Ovid
    Gathered here in this betrayed Court
Of Botticelli's floating
    Only for the young who do not care
For the consequences of plenitude.

Leave it for them and this primavera,
    Swollen, open-mouthed, the smiling cheat struck
    Dumb with the expression of fecundity,
Why the whole party portends movement
    Toward their memorial Italian summer,
These who remain fixed in the postures of seduction.

Please Father, let me spend the summer
    At Urbino...

Like ignored contemporaries
    The voices of the children are long
        Down the halls
            And in the palace
                At Urbino there are volumes
                    Of light, why by the afternoon
                        The air is so thick I have seen
                            Small children float on staircases of it.

As clouds must move everyone is heading
    To the next season on the back of these panels
    The landscape is alive with dogs
Their faces twisted, pit bulls wild as Zephyrus,
    The dogs of caprice and contempt,
    The cannibal dogs, *Connexio Rerum.*

To bite the thigh, devour the heart
    Of the virgin in the forest,
    Chloris stumbles, pursued by the storm
And issues an endless inventory
    Of vines, a chain of cornflowers, gentians, roses
In *The Garden of the Dead*

Here are the leaves of the grape,
   The plant rooted in her heart,
    This too must be an ideal marriage
With the sign of the crow insatiable
    The storm dancing for light
      In the harmony of the memorial summer
        The dogs in the great rooms
          Barking at the sun.

Description of Sea Life

What was it, this crippled half-thing
sidling through thickness, an occasion
for being breathly frail, a glimpse

of an ancient image in an ancient sea,
one more servant in the urge of the world
to move toward something else as though its life
was spent trying to break the surface

where it could never survive alone
and still ascend, I see you ascend
a bridal dress, a headless subject
as though called by another buoy's bell

you would fold in my fist like a white heart,
filmy pump gathering old sea water,
you gather and disperse, gather to disperse
propelling yourself, an invalid organ

in the vital motion of the universe
of nettles, night nettles hundreds rising
through blue plasma, one turns, a medusan head
with cellular hair all in coils,

head or heart you were never the comparison
but the unknown expression about to speak
through the shape of watery human lips.

Justice

for Martin Turner

What are you but a mask of eloquent diction,
of colored print & papier-mâché?
But this is the world's wrapping,
& you, indentured to gratitude,
& gratitude is a loss to memory.

The drapes in the factory worker's home
prevent the view of the factory,
& the subtle fields with the affections
of warmth & color, trees & buds
cover the violence of magma,

it is the body's own organs covered
by flesh that allow any acceptance of them at all.
Justice, you are found in the clothing of the corpse,
arisen from the suffering that is our own,
& from the suffering of others,

to become conscience & conceit.
The brass pole of the pole dancer
is spotted with thumb prints, body grease,
the film of human excrement;
& the derelict on the curb

or office manager, themselves a ruin
of pores, offensive secretions, could never
transcend themselves, & the other masks
to experience clarity, to glide
over the cemeteries of cities,

over inflatable street art, subways,
the unthinkable, but they do,
even in their ruin & in the disintegration of flesh,
the mask itself, and this too
is in the equation of moral physics.

Selbstmord

Sylvia Plath, 1932-1963

Something concurs with the act,
& goes unnoticed like the phantom
that lingers over our decisions
made like bolted horses.

There was more to this than this.

More than vulgar act,
the abandoned children,
more than the flat
without light or heat, the pipes
broken in one of London's
coldest winters, more
than hawkman walking toward Judea,
your fear made flesh,

or the casting away
of a life to punctuate a moment's art,
more than press or biographers say,
more than psychiatry's thinking,
or the stimulation of serotonin,
more than torment of mind,
or the runaway horses running still.

There is more to act than attribution.
There was the knowledge of slipping
into this world among so many
others that could have been,
that are now as we speak, but this one,
this one so rich with invitations—rustling
like spring trees—the anticipation
of the Great Work, the promise
of reunification, the wonderment of affection,
this one requiring obedience to the death notice
posted on our door, through which all
must enter: *von Anfang an und die Quelle.*

It was spirit defiant, spirit resentful,
of the necessary humiliation & remorse.
It was your spirit angered,
yours from the insulted cosmos in you,
from another world saying *nicht mehr,*
saying *dies nicht, dies nicht, dies nicht.*

Glitterati

We are driven by our fascinations.
Glossiness gliding down 5th Avenue,
the imagined life of adulation,
model, saint, club killer.

Arrested by surface attractors,
the impulse is irresistible,
it is what takes the debutante
to the tattoo parlor,

obedience to the magic image;
we are ruled by sparkling things,
like Marilyn in silver lamé
& Arthur with all his shining honors.

The moment of conception was born itself
under the mirrored ball in the dance palace,
replayed in chains of bubbles in countless flutes
of champagne, luminous & effervescent.

The glitterati, hunched over a table,
share the first glint of revolution,
it is all about them.
They toast—a sparkling future.

Gifts

Nature overcompensates:
the dicephalics, for instance,
or those additional vertebrae,
surplus molars, extra digits,
one more finger or toe
just for good measure, and here,
here is another five-chambered heart.

As if there is never enough,
like the patients of good will
who cannot bring enough red wine,
garlic necklaces, daily calendars
with inspirational quotations
given from gratitude,
or admiration, or from the one
last and only hope

they bring other things,
they bring themselves.

It is the excess of the well-intentioned,
the camping outfitter who overfits,
the granger who overfeeds
for a winter that will never come.
The effusions of a heart pumping wildly
behind the heart, with more imagination
than any body can bear.

High Noon at the Stanley

There has been discord traveling
through the mountains
in midsummer, my son
remains in the car, fourteen and angered
by everything. I have crossed
the wide lawn of sculptured light
through the heavy domes of clouds
to a table on the grand porch
with its fluted columns, gold acanthus leaves.

My wife walks the grounds to collect her mind.
The boy is off with a camera to find elk.
We have arrived by troubled coincidence
& exhaustion. Every state has something
like this, a refuge at higher elevations.
Hummingbirds arrive. I consider the menu,
poached salmon, white wine.

Estes Park, a postcard vista, layers
of blue hills falling away into mist,
quiet news of a summer shower later
out on the mountain roads.

My family has been away long enough
I have found time
for a few lines of my own.
The architecture of this hotel
is the architecture of language itself,
a solace of structure, wood & sun,
& all that is outside of this
is the confusion that fails the mind.

The prosperous converse on the lawn,
the best of their day, discussing things,
while their replacements, the student waiters
in white aprons & black ties share plans
for the weekend, as the far trees move

on those blue hills, as those hills themselves move
toward all that is accepted, like Roman stoics
in the light that is hard & cold,
where the best tutors of the speechless live,
where the truly good cannot be tragic.

An Gorta Mor

What is poetry but a mouth,
open & empty like the great hunger,
a mouth with green lips,
stains of vegetation.

When in the Lasting Loveliness of Things

When night calls and you are not to be found,
and when evening stops its descent and is still,
as if waiting for you to appear
before it falls into night once again,

When no thing will turn, not leaves or lovers
in the park, or arise, not breeze or bird,
when these things are still, and waiting for your
return, as if they should never move again

without you, and when I call and call your name
down the empty streets, lined with winter trees,
when all forms have ceased for the sight of you,
for you to arrive and make them possible again—

I have lived my life for this, mine and yours,
in this moment, always before nightfall.

The Doors of Dublin

The doors of Dublin are Georgian doors,
those facing St. Stephen's Green, heavy and wide
and up cold cement steps, each with a brass knocker,
the head of some shining, splendid mythic beast,
Circe, or Siren, or David, or Lion-about-to-speak,
always a single color, solid and bright,
say warm heart-red with white-trimmed fanlight,
night-sky blue, cobalt-dawn, or Kelly green
set in coarsest stone like Dubliners themselves.

Other Acts

After the carnivorous business
was completed out on the savannah
or in elegant suburban bedrooms,
after this, all this
memory forgot, forgave itself once more
as though wantonness & other acts
were sudden rends, small distortions
to say this never really occurred,
to conceal a family disagreement
so the other conversation could continue
like a pair of lovers among ruins
on a wine-colored evening
when all is agreeable & everything
said is certain.

From
ARTIFICIAL LIFE

(BlazeVOX Books, 2009)

Flyleaf

Nothing collapses so easily
in the fist than this,
the onion skin that crinkles
like the sound of the word, creation.

It is the twig that bows
in the wind & sweeps over the forearm,
or the peach that brushes
against the peach,

& these are found in pages
as if among a feathery crowd
of angels jostling in awe
toward the next wonder just ahead.

There, with all the round syllables,
the rustlings of a world
trying to fill us with sense
again.

Not about This

It is not about the classic rivers
of mythology, not about Acheron,
river of woe with its lines of unemployed
holding their migraines in their hands.

Or Cocytus, river of lamentation
where the elderly have gone
to grieve their condition.

It cannot be this.

Not the river of fire,
the lava flowing from another volcanic shudder
into the homes of the living & the dead,
& into the stories of new generations.

For these are by-products,

shining as they are—

It is not about the river of forgetfulness,
inviting as the night visits the tortured mind.
No, not this, or the waters of hate
& the butchered bodies stacked along shorelines
& the lost women trying to find their sons,

or the river of return,

not the red river of consolation
wound about the heart
& through the vineyards,
or how our loves came to be,
then left us again to ourselves.

It is not about the oldest & saddest river,
the river of time, with flashes of metallic film
sliding by gathering momentum,
& the surfaces of faces,
the faces of phantoms
(I have seen myself among them).

It cannot be about classical dramaturgy,
or if it is, it is the dramaturgy of celestial mechanics,
the giant narrative of everything,
the source of energy (& its forms)
crunching itself out through the heavens.

Artificial Life

All performances today have been cancelled.

Make no mistake. There must be nothing
out of the ordinary, it's been posted,
no marching, we must stand fast.
The myth of the exploding star
and the next extinction have been
put on hold wherever you are
it too has been, innocence and the isolation
of the justice gene, the paper cutout
on Valentine's Day underscoring
the shadowy lattice and blue thatch
that came with the biothermal work,
day labor grinding away again
without the special knowledge of anyone
not even the curators of armies
like the pencil sketches they made
of dark figures hiding in cellars,
no one in particular, going where they are
going, and the part-time return, agitated
about the revisions, the supreme biological
auction and the disagreeing classes of thought,
the grumbling forces, but they've been
shut down, as we speak, even the factories
across the street have closed for the day
until we get it straight, which cannot occur
because of all the new business coming to the valley
and all the others who remain uninformed.

Commentary on Multiple Systems

What brought them here was essential
as the variations of opinions themselves,
as chaos & harmony working through other lives
in distant regions at once & also in classes
of this time, in salons with walls
of metallic leaf, thin iridescent lavas
from deposits of common speech. They advance.

Near a parked car an argument breaks out
as others gather in the public park, an affair
under the moon my neighbor admires the iris garden
& for the present forgives loss & extravagance
in bubbling pools, in the cause of the general course
it is the night of the one shooting star.
The sky is clear as gratitude.

The spectacular, sought by a diverse group has broken
off from the party on the next block to form its own,
a commotion coming down my street, the numb rustle
of indigo silk, a train of fluttering things
collecting followers on the way in a movement
that pulls them past the street light, past the windows
of neighbors—gowns float wide as invitations;

Newcomers spread the word & leave the exhausted
on the curb with the burned-out casings
of railyard flares, sparkling paper hats,
the iris gardener can no longer resist the park,
& the other groups, attracted & ignored divide again,
gain momentum, spilling over themselves
effusive as cool lava out onto night highways.

Fireflies at Harsens Island

The group and the group leader said the wind
would never come to this town or to this,
so it was up & down the seaboard
until it was dead, dead as the basin
of human opinion, dead as the port
of Ephesus, dead as the once sacred
society that would survive it all,
its bright flags flying over the purpose.

    Word went out. In the yellow oily smear
    of midsummer's most profuse sunflowers
    they came from every county in the state,
    took ferries, came as far as Ohio
    to join the local farm families even on foot
    from the bar *Sans Souci* with their evening
    partners they came, with busloads of seniors
    to gather in the fields for nightfall & fairy light.

It would never happen again, not like this,
& it did not happen, so they settled in
for their stay—the immediate signal:
the popular ode turning on itself
like a leaf, a dove's wing, the wind dipping
into the waters of old ports & clouds
like the colonnades of Smyrna shifting
to accommodate them, for those few

    who alerted others, altering them,
    blips like the shouts of city boys
    at summer camp into the dark meadows,
    the bending neon silos, the ballrooms
    with balconies of bright ideas,
    dithyramb of lantern-glow, cold sulphur
    spirals of nymphs performing in the shapes
    of their shapes, heads filled with divine objects,

one moved forward into the immense dark
as Zelus was led past the port & the last
sphere of influence, forsaking all others

on the journey of no return, the bold
voice exchanged for a dawn of ghosts,
they returned to Bar Harbor, Twin Rivers,
the one fawn-eyed farm boy with the fruit jar
lantern & seniors in their gilded buses.

Minor Figures

To land
            once again among giants

with the composure of a feather in blind trust
the wedding photo of my parents was taken in a vestry
so the day began with the certainty of new cloth,

& father who did not care for Masaccio
& refused to travel by air
stood innocent of the pillars filled with forty
years of Detroit factory whistles & steam
enough to melt summer streets.

In the shadow of the square
against the church of Milan
an acrobat like a stunned frog flipped in midair
performs for admirers of window models
in winter coats who hold dusty bottles
of flower water, for those who could not know

        the shadow of the length of the tower
        is the exact length of all returnings.

Again the steel feather cuts the scar tissue,
runs down the seam of the church like a zipper
so the summer asphalt is heavy with anise.

From an aerial view the minutiae scutter
five miles below in their own culture,
the Congo or the forests of Lombardy—

In his desperate whisper as with cigarette stains mounting
the wallpaper, the elevator operator says "Come marry me,
marry me," all day long
sending up compartments of rattling coat hangers.

Something Left for Others

You said everything I wanted to hear
maybe all that could be said at the time,
   the troubled boys in gangs going door to door,
   adolescent sweethearts showing up
from the party at midnight, tired, wandering
   off again, from the beginning, on the snowy

day we first met indoors, it was unavoidable
   as this conversation, and later
when we both moved it was difficult to keep
in touch, but you did all you were able to do,
   the glimpse between the passenger trains,
this much was clear, there was the presence

   of others, maybe you needed them here
as if it had become too much, like rates
   of interest, an unending mortgage,
   too much for you alone, the responsibility
of outsized landfills, the requirement of others
   to attend—you did all you were able to do.

Raccoon Feeding in the Gold Run Dumpsters

What actually occurred cannot be known,
not even for another language   before dawn

magpies rushed the parking lot
below my bedroom window, a council
disputing territory, food sources,
the morality of disequilibrium
on the metallic film of the asphalt
squawking through the unknown terror
which had the residents trapped inside
staring out the windows
for the duration of the neurological storm,
eternal funeral begun with the magpies
coming, a family of raccoons waddled
into the scene, out for gourmet dining,
bandits of the garbage heap, nosing around
through bottles and cans for chicken bones,
bits of pie crust, always chittering
as they do, I pulled myself to the deck,
pitched stones which made no difference,
they went on until dawn, woke my son
who moaned, & at this hour another subject
of the gene of dread, with the cantings of the magpies
& coons & my own unknown event
entered in my muddy notebook, the stones gone,
I returned to bed, the world resumed
its conference uncertain as I was
the wind picked up leaning into a forecast
of early showers among cloudy pillars.

Urban Development

The field is cleared, is cleared
clear of trees torn up
cleared of stumps blown out—

before we came to the explosions
with words that signify no object
the impact was realized
& is realized as the field is cleared
with the velocity that sent us off
in the convolutions of our means
as if they were equal to those
that surround us
those that will invade us—

what builder would consider
the development as grounded
in the flash over the field?

& now, just as we are convinced
the field is contained
the edge dissolves toward us

The Carmine Cycle

i

The firebirth of the female cochineal
extinguishes the water
moving like the pattern of a waltz.

ii

The limits of observation have forced
the diffusion of the question
in the pronoun of the cochineal
whose imperial theme is the color
that consumes the astronomer's clock
thrown out in the middle,
Wednesday walking into rainy Wednesday.

iii

Limitless they are, the limited
frames lining the lake,
a chenille panorama
where iron microbe & micron meet,
rust out another gender.

iv

This compression of gestures
mimes the miniature conch directing
the movement of a waltz
on a floor that is not flat,
learning the box step we practice variations
to dusty draperies, the gray & endless morning street—

Sunday Picnic

A postscript: I saw the storm
    rise over the lake,
    you left the scene,
    walked off into the tall grasses blowing

which has led me to this:

if reason is white like the anger of the knuckle
    & desire drips valentine red
    spread like a tablecloth on the lawn
then all the signs & tissues of substance
    give every expression a form
    & every form its idea of expression,

as bubbles rise from fishes' mouths,

the world of water & the world of air
    melodic as grass or cloud or moving star,
    the great hatcheries of the night glitter with scales
like a tablecloth rippling in summer wind.

Lines on a Dog's Face

Wallace said what the eye beholds may be
the text of life, & in this case it is
the Springer, Cynthia, whose eyes
are the brown corridors of vacuity,
moral deserts where the absolute Nothing
is, or nothing but her repetitions,
the fence-line patrol, the daily quarrels
with the cat, begging always for scraps
& a nap to sleep it off, then waiting
alert for something to be known.

Agent of operation, living primordium,
memoir of Something clearly in her stare
which would say only, "I have known this
for a very long time," retriever
of the stick locked in crocodile teeth,
living the life of the fanciful
scenario, chasing doves, the evening
meal, her wrinkles busily playing
out a program, a contemporary opinion,
the repetitions that govern her earth, & mine.

Epistemology

There could have been other scenes as well
as these, by way of the flame or the forest,
or say, iris and calla lily, but the range was set,
the discursive mandalas of book clubs,
arcologies, the long miles
of mental villages along the riverbanks
that are always changing—
what were we ever trying to make
of the waters' patterns and its confluences—
the doxology of the dream
to which we surrendered every ounce of belief
only to leave it for another
like an unfaithful lover
behind the scenes,
multiple courtships in the same house—
strangers to each other,
more visitors to the central library—

if only we had more time to read.

Salton Sea

It is the purest body
of sensation, the heavy
liquid shrine of saline
& by all rights should have died
long ago & instead found
the essence of composition,
pale, complete, surrounded,
where bleached light & water join
blandness & a climate formed
a resting place for the winded
creatures of the Pacific
Flyway, Arctic gulls & white
endangered pelicans, those
yet to be identified
bobbing on the warm water
below sea level, a place
of convalescence, vacant,
full of things that are
& are not wavering in the purest
forms imaginable.

Departure

The other self, the one that speaks would say
I am seen only now as myself,
as I am leaving, over & over
again to all I have ever known,
to what makes leaving possible,
a practice, the letting go, to move without,
to move along the slopes of another
place where I remain more & more myself,
elevated, unexplained.

Burial Ground, Index of Renunciations

For what was never known & still known,
what was teased away, taken, distracted
elsewhere, whorls of nightsteam assembled
in the unexpected, the unkept schedule
the next flitting combination
of trellis shadow & cloud shadow
& the winter branch across a white porch

diverted, for the thing that almost was,
that never reached the ledge of the language
of itself, for the extensions that floated
about a shape from lambent torsion sprung,
raided by other tensions, for movements
of the imagined, for the unseen lives
of their expressions

which go off without us, outside of the few
things of the conscious mind, for the always-
occurring to reveal some strand, tincture,
the copper-peach reflections on an evening
puddle, some patch or section for the poem
that attempted these things,
for its abode of longing,

the brick school in the wet morning,
for the act that concurs with every other act
of disclosure, for the life crisscrossed
with these, for the soul of one night
full of itself, requiring nothing,
for the perpetual cancellations of experience,
for their coilings,

unformed destinies winding through metal groves,
for the renunciations themselves,
for the fields of reported flowers,
suggestions half-made, caught, hand over mouth,
for the replacements, for what was found
least & most, inadequate, removed,
for all things then, for ourselves.

The Mathematics of Adoration

The pink geranium reflected in the glass
of the patio table will never be
as intense as it is this moment
when it is perfect
as a ring of words
that has no counterpart beyond itself
as the flower is this moment a reflection
of itself, fire-pressed in glass & all
other things that are precisely now.

The Tropic Gardens of St. Gallen

Were done with old dreams
sagging like vines after winter

sinew-netted the ruins
Roman or Swiss crowd the mild day
subjects of impatience
spring, statues tighten
with passion flowers

like elongated hands
sought in the dark
approaching the gables
of disfigured hunters and porous fawns
above the pillars and the checked parquet
tiles of another setting the night brought
from its changing geometry

and we walked among them
as though to discover at last
what intricacy our walking would bring

to perform the great task
we imagined perfection
so we would always seek it

the gardens of language

and turned away toil spent
like the widow's silk on the cornices at Tivoli
or the willows of Chapultepec

companion, talking with your hands
under the dry trellis
in your winter blanket and mountain chair
you have been faithful to the world

to the gables
the Alpine gables

Pregnant Girl on the Genesee River Bridge

I have taken a bench on the bridge
my parents walked when courting
under the shadow of the Times-Square
building in downtown Rochester.

The city scene is gray, intentional, a mini Gotham,
the waters of the Genesee slow & dirty-green,
shallow & fetid, where I've come out
once again to greet the evening.

And she appears, a child herself
carrying another under the faded rainbow
tank top stretched tight & stained, she leans
against the heavy railing and stares at the water.

High above the white gulls fly
toward the great lake. They use the river
as a guide, like a line on an aerial map,
& the child smiles at me, once, turns away & sighs.

What is here is here & what has gone has gone.
Under the steel towers, under the statue of Mercury,
the brick & glass looming over the bridge,
such ruins among such strong forms.

Best Said

Some things are best left unsaid,
    the long-term promises of lovers,
    the life one wished one would have led.

Other things are better left unread,
    tomorrow's obituary, the bad review,
    the things about us others said.

Some things are better left undone,
    the great project that could never be,
    misunderstood by nearly everyone.

Some things are better left with the dead,
    so much of what is best said
    dies with its owners, unloved, unread.

From
SURFACES

(March Street Press, 2006)

Bridge at Giverny

In pursuit of the changing subject Monet
Wanted to paint the air, the air he breathed
Inhaling images of bridges
Gold boats shimmering buildings bloated he became
A cloud among clouds over his ponds,
A reflection in a world of reflections
Imagining itself...

Imagining paint flecks in the nervous light,
Fleck after fleck, a water music, the music
That breathes with perception
As with ether or alcohol to take the breath away
And the suggestion of the lines they make
Distorted as though day and night conspire
To take objects from a clearer sight
To place them with the unknown
In absence of both dark and bright

Reflections among surfaces, light on water
Wavering the look of the moon, the thin
Continents on which we drift,
To live the life of dimension,
A religion of surfaces, Monet's vest,
The sides of the human face, its clothing of flesh,
Looking at the sky in the ponds at Giverny
On Monet's bridge I stood moving
Among surfaces, worlds of surfaces.

This Evening

This evening in the copper-plated autumn,
it must be a comfort to know
there is one center to all things.

Still, I cannot make a statement
that does not carry a remark inside,
that would emerge outward as a conical shape
from a frame. I cannot make a statement
that does not listen
to itself, even as it is being made.

I have leaned against the doorway
where the suction draws up
the last weak fever, evaporates itself
then snaps back the copper screen
with copper-plated hinges.

Why I recall the man myself, take just one
step backward and saw him still
standing in the doorway.

Peninsular Storm

The wind is full of will
along the coast of the Gaspé,
battering the white shacks
of the native population.

It will not allow another language
& turns sharply taking the breath away,
out to sea...

The gray gathers, effusive
as Greco's winter sky
far out to sea
another image has been drawn
across the water
to collapse about the single pine
full of rain.

Red Deer Rock

Driving north of Gallup where nothing
Is expected, where nothing
But the hot silence of the desert
Penetrates the pastel sand,
So pale appearing
Transparent,
Even an insect, a fly perhaps
Would be a welcome companion

In the monotony of too much expanse
A red deer congealed in an instant
And jumped out from the embankment
Suspended in air
Like a Christmas reindeer
Then the paralysis disappeared
And in a blink, was gone...

I concluded such transient
Apparitions make poor companions
Before I saw its shadow painted on the sand.

A World without Desire

Occurred tonight for an hour only,
An hour spent around the back porch
Where I was sent from the family, exiled
From myself. It was a world of order,
Order and presence, the final meaning
Of forms conversing through the night
As large as all thought must be
This house a ragged piece of locale
Torn and adrift in the space of a dark mind.

Every variety of matter floats by,
The blue-silver dust motes of the moon,
Distant lights of unidentifiable aircraft,
Colored, small as fireflies
In the tilted sheet of my cigar smoke,
Vegetable flakes, dried insects' wings,
Luminous bits of debris, fanciful nuclei
Circling themselves like smiling opinions
Without destinations, souls that surround

And surround their forgotten voyages,
Sparks from a funeral fire sucked whirling
In a draft, a cigar coal added
To this effluvium of references
Describing presence by glimmering
Forms only, no destiny other than a world
Without desire, a world without end,
A description I could take inside
Long after the family retired.

Einstein's Last Words

As she had the wheel, I could relax,
Stare up at the sky, its blueness
Everywhere, an ascending dome of blue
Absence, an awareness of space alone,
The formless, what it is to be
Detached at eleven thousand feet crossing
Wolf Creek Pass over the Continental
Divide in the cool, placid blue
As though the calling and the thing

Called were consumed at the moment
Experiencing itself
I saw the stand of Aspen shimmer once
Like a large shoulder chilled
By the mountain breeze, a goddess leaving
The scene to the Aspen that did nothing
But introduce a horse in a meadow,
Its head bowed, staring as if occupied
With some dim glimmering of being,

The flickering of a leaf turned by the breeze
Called to observe its own absence only,
To memorize itself as this, a pause
While dying for everything
In spring among pools of snow wash,
The popular meadows, the reflective
Sky, and the horse struck out of the blue.
It is the problem of identity,
We must live in the houses of others,

I say to my wife, now driving slowly
As we near the summit—this is why
The insane were called holy,
Why the meek will inherit the earth.
When the weather was cold we slept,
Perhaps there is an ultimate climate
Of being, *Ens Parmenideum*, the source
Of speculation, of the softer creatures
And other significant works of the world—

On his deathbed, Einstein mumbled
To his nurse in German, a language
She did not understand, maybe it was
Another formula to disclose the universe,
Or in the confusion of his last moments
He thought she was there to take his order
And he said—I want fish—
With his doleful expression, then stared past her,
Past the furnishings, across the room
Distracted, once again.

Copland at Chautauqua

The earlier movements were so still
They could not be heard, not by outsiders
Who drifted in among elms
With bottles and baskets. They spread blankets
Under the dull blue evergreens
Swaying heavily and it was obvious
From the start how they approved
Of everything, even the waiting
Outside the barnwood auditorium,
It was all it was ever supposed to be,
The birds gliding on the silver sheen
Among the poplars on the hill, the lyrical
Merlot curving in a glass, how they smiled
On themselves, on their admiration,
On what brought this Appalachian Spring,
The intervals that became an evening,
A trend, in unison they smiled on the score
Of incidentals that created the occasion,
The trees, the admirers, this composer,
That chamber, that all this
May have happened without them,
Or just as easily with others
As they smiled on the sheen among clouds,
The breeze, the smell of perfume, their own
Earthly smell, deciduous, the same,
The odor of sanctity, and beyond
Bear grass and sea grass in July the woman
At the roadside gate in her print dress
With her little boy waving good-bye and good-bye,
The impressions they wished to make.

Floral Arrangement for a New Species

Recently arrived in the mix
Of things, like a memory
   Pushing itself through
      All others, as if unrelated
         Only to hear its welcome
            By little hands in a white garden
               Clapping like petals

Although they are still.
It is now in the braid of things,
   In with the one voice
      Of the world's youngest soprano
         On the television in the room
            Behind me, through the screen door
               Of the deck where I am surrounded

By floating cottonwood fluff
That sticks to my hair, the back
   Of my neck in the late spring
      With the mountain thunder
         Like applause from a wedding
            Where everyone is
               A spouse, bride and bridegroom,

Guest and owner,
The unrecognized plot
   In showers of puff-seed
      A fresh shape come
         From its ethereum, blossom
            Of white lilac, enough to fill
               The hand's cup like a small breast.

Frida

You are dancing with Diego
in the courtyard of the blue house.

Your painted record is not so clear,
the self-portraits for example,
the martyred stag shot full of arrows,
heads sprouting from other heads
& the signature of that browline
(an exaggeration from your photographs)
conjoins itself like the outrageous wings
of a dark baby bird
fixed between your eyes.

Factory of body parts,
machine of flesh,
I do not believe you
painted yourself for pity.

I do not believe you
displayed your broken self
to show your other body

in holy allegory. Your eyes are too hard
for that. They are hard & black
& refractive. Everything is sent back.

You are yourself a gathering
of facts, that is not wholly victim art,
broken column, twisted umbilicus,
dead fetus against the soot stacks of Detroit,
rusted blood, exposed arteries & heart,
those querulous monkeys on your back—

When you hold hands with your lover
yourself—in the portrait of your two bodies,
a political gesture, the divides
of culture & sex, a union
of split identity
as if the column created
you too

& a vanishing twin
that switches bodies,
& love, like a third eye
remains to watch
loyalty's nervous twitch.

Frida, I want to go on with you.
I do.

But you are too difficult for me.

In my heart
I know you are insatiable.

It is late. It was already too late
for this.

The last image, biographers say,
when you bolted upright
during cremation, your hair burning
like a halo, & your lips
turning back in a macabre smile
beyond any statement
of generation or party—

So I must leave you, Frida,

dancing with Diego
in the courtyard of the blue house.

From
EARTHLY BODIES

(Pudding House Publications, 2004)

Anorexic Student

I cannot find the voice for you,
Something left unsaid, impossible
In your presence, culture-bound to vogue,
The central attraction of runway values,
The tights and blouse that cling
To the contours of bone, sharp ridges
Of hips, the pubic mound are Christian Dior.
The pouty mouth dry from crystal meth,
What you take in your defense,
A charmed life of sea kelp and spritzers
With the rest of an airy world
Through palpy lips, vulnerable
Vortex of sex, beauty, and early death.

You bring your papers to my desk
With eyes moody, promiscuous
And leave with an endless line of boys
To be controlled, spent, then sent away
In your search for the perfect cure
Which somehow always returns to pain.
The golden image of the golden girl
With skin cool, marmoreal, you turn
To say "I'm sorry," once again.

The black hollow eyes of marble Greeks
Through which the world is said to stare
Are yours, product of consumer culture,
First to be consumed,
Your eyes grow dark, you descend
Past anything that would have led
To self-discovery, flesh following flesh.

I cannot speak for you.
You will remain your wish,
Something left unsaid,
Obsessive image, in five years
At the outside by physician's count
Those studio teeth will calcify

Hard as stone—the heart gone—
And I will insist I have some voice
In the matter, asking
For what you would only scorn,
Some small honor grieving still.

Short History of Opera

The society of experience
Speaks also, an anthology
Of learnèd ones who have taken
Their complaints outside
Like a collection of patients
On the grounds of the state facility,
Or in Merz's *Asylum,* where each group
Itself is in another engraving,
A composition of graphic sound.

In the holy history of the downfallen
There is the ancestral moan, a constant
Background to our daily affairs
Where the innocence of actors—the farmer
Who thinks he's a farmer, the brooding
Mother of course, old politician,
Barefoot writer in stocking cap—
Becomes larger now for sorrow,
Made so by this, who, after their air-bath
And reflections move quietly inside
And pray nightly for a transformation
That will occur and not be known.

A Visitation to the Smallest of Words

It stormed again last night. Cemented things,
    The stadium and the parking lot are still wet.

The landscape blurs, just as it did
    When our eyes watered. Colored spears
        A lens of fictions. No thing was memorable.

Only some vague experience, an occurrence,
    The emergence of occasions for others—

The night was clear, balmy. You complained
    Of a sore throat. The weather. A souvenir
        From the night air.

What things you were, what things,
    The smallest of words.

Genii Loci

There must be other inhabitants of the places
We attend, enough to animate us surely
With some residue, why else would we spend
Our lives among ruins? Why would we seek
Out city museums on rainy days?
What is the central attraction
Of country villas, the roofless homes
Of abandoned towns, empty doorways,
Those painted caves of Altamira
With their remains of ancient fires?

Why this fall did we drive for hours
To see the colors? How many deep groves
Of evergreen, stands of Aspen and bright
Birch called to us like memory itself
Standing among them spellbound with leaves
Clicking like the dry tongues of prior knowledge?
It must be so. Why would we have stepped
Between mounds of sacred information
In remote cemeteries to trace
Headstones with charcoal as if to reclaim

Enough of those figures who at last
Would lead us to the place these places made.

To What Attends Moving Forms

From the knowledge of small things:

Something then gin-clear, lighter-than-air
Occurring with moving forms
Spinning drake, night-chime
Wind-spool, water-wake,
Lavender-breath among the lavender.

From objects, the invisible issues
Invading epochs, sight lines, more—
What is held is held for something else,
Earth bedrock for ocean, ocean for air
Air for bird-flight, contours
Of soil, vessels for landscapes,
Cervix, vase & valley, instrument
Case, coliseum, voice box, cranium, cortex,
Cortex & lie, flowers
And morning rain—
And still others unseen, next & neighboring.

What is by movement made
Wavering heat off sill & runway
Seen through jet fuel,
An appearance through objects—
Prescient dogs, earth's quake.

Interview with Ovid

Up all night, glassy-eyed,
Nervous he speaks quickly
Saying how the yellow catclaw
On the garden wall and the pink oleander
Recombine themselves. His feet dirty
& ankles swollen—"I have thirty seconds
With every poet in the universe,
Even with Eumenes, even with
The sub-minors of the lesser anthology,"
Declines my invitation to dinner,
Critiques my work saying I crossed
The lines, then steps back among the shades,
His figure wavy & watery
Among the leaves of my fig tree,
Saying we could trade places,
Saying this even as he was disappearing.

Fiddlers at the Desert Valley County Care Center

Among physicians rich in their death watch
In hallways crowded with locked wheelchairs,
Cradles of a century's platitudes,
The stale air smelling of disinfectant
And weeping wounds enough to stupefy nurses,
Among the staring insomniacs of the day room,
The stroke victims on their rented gurneys,
Complaining orderlies and rattling carts

Among these in this place my father lay
At the end of everything

In the curved landscapes of white sheets
Abandoned finally by parents, his son,

The loyal company, old friends, his death
A sign of other deaths too soon to come

Unable to recall one life, his thoughts,
Features, he lay unknown to himself,

The tall hunter of pheasants out with his boy
In vellum corn and brassy orchards

In an autumn that never was, the proud
White-collared Ford employee lay on a bed

Too short for legs tattooed with red burn-rings
From daily syringes of Cytosar

Considered useless, still a requirement
For state funding for a body described

Leukemic waiting for Saturday's fiddlers
Who came to raise the spirits of the dead

With a music he never cared for turned
Suddenly attractive, he found genius,

Theirs or his like some lyrical phosphor
That shapes itself in the dry night air

To make a thing then make it disappear
He lay listening to the county fiddlers

At the end of every purpose, act and form
I leave you here, my father, in perfect accord.

Signs of Importance

We had the best of everything.
It was true, the traces of peach
On the summer air, a balance
Among the higher reaches, the arbors
Just touching over the last long street of leaves—

Elements stable as the century
Itself, everyone agreed on the events,
How the crowds raved at the concert—
Even the dialects were the same, what could be
Better? We understood propriety

Yesterday, it rained. It rained on the houses
And on the leafy streets, it may be
Raining still. The mailboxes dissolved.
The whole postal system, like certitude itself
Collapsed. Signatures ran from bundles of wet letters.

The curious watched high fashion put off
On its memorial cruise, enemies became heroes
Overnight, as for myself, I looked for my neighbors,
Migrations were moving to the next magnetic field
And the new registry didn't have a single reference for you.

Death Wish

"Those troubled toes, loops of early white hair,
Green eyes and what Irish you have were gifts
From your mother," she said, failing to note
The other, the fatal kiss, the cymbals' clash
To conclude the circus of arteries
(Playing on through generations of family),
Her ticket to Dublin redeemed one afternoon
While resting on a couch of peach brocade
When father stepped out for a few things,
For tea and bread and aspirin, for absence,
And returned never to forgive himself.
"Some die in sleep, they really do,"
She informed her only child from boyhood—
Repetition will make a romance true.

When my mother's final gift is given,
(An aneurysm no doubt, now once said
And out of mouth, I will likely tumble
A summer tourist from a ski lift,
Or from a collection of rare cancers),
Best to be swept in sleep from the same
Peach couch kept in my living room,
An occasional piece, and my ashes
Dusted over the quad where the spring
Girls come to sit and read and speak
And speaking low a gold mote might be inhaled
Or otherwise absorbed, the barest
Modicum of dust reformed there
On the green lawn of my alma mater.

Repose

This house is a museum of others,
Other possessions, the walls wear
The signs of life. They breathe—
A gallery of essential things,
Dried flowers in frames, miniature spoons,
Shadow boxes of anniversaries, thimbles,
A tile-chip, Registry Room, Ellis Island,
Souvenirs of sentimental journeys,
The gold-plated ashtray from the World's Fair
Each one the perfect thing that could not be
Remembered, the souls of human experience,
Glassed linen doilies snatched from the chairs
Of the dead, where they once rested
Surrounded by other lives, dreamed
Of the departed as though to make them
Their own, the things they were we are
Or try to be and we look on these
As we would look on the hearts of heaven.

Curator of the repository, I have gone
To estate sales, second-hand stores at night
To rescue the damned, just one more
Ghost Ranch with translucent sheep
And dissolving sky to mix with my wife's
Watercolors of abandoned farms, a reprieve
Before they pass again into the hands
Of strangers, themselves borrowers,
Then sold, misplaced, discarded, lost,
An oak box clock smelling of lemon oil
That resonates on the hour with arguments
And the exclamations of its owners,
A mandolin, my father's teak table,
Closets full of suits, cleaned, in plastic bags
Hung like the bodies of past relatives
To these we add a few things of our own,
My wife's art, my room of poems, this house itself
An abode of souls inhabited now by others.

Night Watch

There was something else I wanted to say
    But it is gone now, blown out into the field,
    Joined up with the wind, another marriage
Running around doing the impossible,
    Or maybe it disappeared to the basement
In the Museum of Postmodern Man

Among recesses, in a portico
    That has disposed itself of models
    And has nothing left to go on, not even
The civilization outside, the one
    That took up with the wind
Like the voices of everyone talking

Out the solution—maybe it was you,
    The poem of oblivion, or another
    Sensation in the Retrospective
Of Queer Ideas, wearing thin
    As the sole of the watchman's shoe
Padding down halls trying to find someone special.

UNCOLLECTED POEMS

(2016)

To History—

You will not remember me.
And I will not remember you.
So while we are keeping company
please note the blue delphinium
climbing past the window.

Braidings

When the surf at Laguna Beach recedes,
it leaves a pattern in the sand, long braids
of Xs, a net over the beach that fades
to flatness with the next wave
and is made again when the ocean draws back,
as if the water is writing itself.

Among bulbs of amber kelp that pop
underfoot, among castaways, fragments
of driftwood, tentacles of seaweeds,
ocean's excrement, darling detritus
of former generations, now hosts
for a thousand organisms, the dog's

plump paw prints and my footprints mix,
withdraw in recessions of bubbling foam.
How we return to waters, how the subject
is in us, the heart's whoosh and the wave's,
the tang of saline on lips or tongue,
the Xs of waves' writing never done.

***

This is the morning of my seventieth year.
It began clearly, without meditation,
until I saw the water's writing on the sand
and waded out in the surf as far as we dared,
the dog barking at sea birds, then searching
the water for some lost fish it might rescue

by dragging it to shore. Just this past summer
my son and I drifted nine miles down the Platte,
past pelicans on shoals, our boat followed
by antelopes along the sandy bluffs,
and when we noticed other waterways weaving
in and out like trances, and asked their names

as they were rivers too, the guide said all
were nameless, as they were braids, some
from the Platte, others that joined in—and out,

still others that sprung up and made their journeys,
too many to count or know, their weavings
forming confluences and tail waters

where fish gathered, weaving in schools,
in currents subtle and muscular, themselves
plaiting with the fish. In another summer
I saw the streams of the Cotswolds
swaying with bands of algae, cadmium green,
drifting among swans, in motions perpetual.

***

Later, after our surf-walk, the dog asleep
in the hotel room, I went to the rooftop lounge
of Casa del Camino where servers, the Laguna girls
with golden braids, seemed to float from table to table,
and thus the music of hair, an almost impossible
music to bear, for what was left of such bodies

of brine but traces of salt weavings, outlines,
found in the making of paper and glass,
in mirrors, as if suffering purifies form
and, meanwhile, how our fingers intertwined,
how our nomad bodies curved
into each other, into our braiding selves.

Acknowledgments

Grateful acknowledgment is made to the following publications in which some of these poems first appeared:

10x3 plus: "Salton Sea," "Departure," "Utility," "Flyleaf," "Best Said"
The American Literary Review: "Rites of Spring"
Ann Arbor Review: "Moonstruck," "Poem"
Atticus Review: "Minor Figures"
The Aurorean: "Pregnant Girl on the Genesee River Bridge"
The Blue Guitar Magazine: "Letter to a Poet" "Père Lachaise," "Rain," "The Return"
Buffalo Spree Magazine: "Carmine Cycle," "Peninsular Storm," "Red Deer Rock," "Ineffable Conversations," "This Evening," "Urban Development"
Byline Magazine: "A Visitation to the Smallest of Words," "Canticle, Poet-Anima"
Cavalier Literary Couture: "The Keys of Paris," "Six Spanish Girls on the Streets of Cambridge"
Chiron Review: "Einstein's Last Words," "Night Watch"
Eclipse: "Promiscuity"
The French Literary Review: "Le Moulin de la Vierge," "Place des Vosges"
Glimpse (Toronto): "Voltaire's Cap"
JAMA: The Journal of the American Medical Association: "Anorexic Student," "Gifts"
Nimrod International Journal of Prose and Poetry: "Thoth," "Seshat"
North American Review: "Sex Education," "To History—" (a finalist for the 2016 James Hearst Poetry Prize)
Nimrod International Journal of Prose and Poetry: "Thoth," "Seshat"
Oxford Magazine: "Lines on a Dog's Face" (reprinted in *Dog Music,* St. Martin's Press)
Pacific Review (20th Anniversary Edition): "Ferns: A Study"
Paterson Literary Review: "Winter Reading"
Poem: "Bridge at Giverny," "SundayPicnic," "White Doors"
Rue des Beaux-Arts (Paris): "Wilde's Tomb"
Sycamore Review: "The Tropic Gardens of St. Gallen"
Verse-Virtual: "Petit Cailloux," "The Innocents at Sandy Hook," "Boy in a Boat," "Poem," "The Poem of Death"
The Wallace Stevens Journal: "A World without Desire" (reprinted in *Poet's Market,* Writer's Digest Books, 1993-1997 editions)
Web del Sol: "Artificial Life," "Not about This"

Windhover: "Genii Loci"
Wisconsin Review: "Description of Sea Life," "Other Acts"
The Yale Journal for Humanities in Medicine: "Washed Out"

"Selbstmord" and "I Had Your Book" were selected as finalists by the judges
of the monthly poetry contest hosted by Goodreads.com. "The Keys of Paris"
and "The Doors of Dublin" were recorded in radio broadcast (KXCI-Tucson,
February 20, 2012). "Departure" was composed by invitation for the painting
of the same title by Laura den Hertog, which appeared as the cover image of
10x3 plus(2008). The pairing of graphite sculptured hearts by Dalton Ghetti
and the poem, "The Keys of Paris," by the editors of *LitCouture.* "Magnificat"
appeared in *Verse Daily* (July 6, 2014).

*Cover image of staircase from the public domain; cover and interior book design
by Diane Kistner; Gentium Book Basic text and Cronos Pro titling*

About FutureCycle Press

FutureCycle Press is dedicated to publishing lasting English-language poetry books, chapbooks, and anthologies in both print-on-demand and Kindle ebook formats. Founded in 2007 by long-time independent editor/publishers and partners Diane Kistner and Robert S. King, the press incorporated as a nonprofit in 2012. A number of our editors are distinguished poets and writers in their own right, and we have been actively involved in the small press movement going back to the early seventies.

The FutureCycle Poetry Book Prize and honorarium is awarded annually for the best full-length volume of poetry we publish in a calendar year. Introduced in 2013, our Good Works projects are anthologies devoted to issues of universal significance, with all proceeds donated to a related worthy cause. Our Selected Poems series highlights contemporary poets with a substantial body of work to their credit; with this series we strive to resurrect work that has had limited distribution and is now out of print.

We are dedicated to giving all of the authors we publish the care their work deserves, making our catalog of titles the most diverse and distinguished it can be, and paying forward any earnings to fund more great books.

We've learned a few things about independent publishing over the years. We've also evolved a unique, resilient publishing model that allows us to focus mainly on vetting and preserving for posterity poetry collections of exceptional quality without becoming overwhelmed with bookkeeping and mailing, fundraising activities, or taxing editorial and production "bubbles." To learn more about what we are doing, come see us at www.futurecycle.org.

The FutureCycle Poetry Book Prize

All full-length volumes of poetry published by FutureCycle Press each calendar year are considered for the annual FutureCycle Poetry Book Prize. This allows us to consider each submission on its own merits, outside of the context of a contest. Too, the judges see the finished book, which will have benefitted from the beautiful book design and strong editorial gloss we have become famous for.

The book ranked the best in judging is announced as the prize-winner in the subsequent year. There is no fixed monetary award; instead, the winning poet receives an honorarium of 20% of the total net royalties from all poetry books and chapbooks the press sold online in the year the winning book was published. The winner is also accorded the honor of being on the panel of judges for the next year's competition; all judges receive copies of all contending books to keep for their personal libraries.

www.ingramcontent.com/pod-product-compliance
Lightning Source LLC
Chambersburg PA
CBHW072142090426
42739CB00013B/3259